Teddy Roosevelt

A Captivating Guide to the Life of Theodore Roosevelt Who Served as the 26th President of the United States of America

© Copyright 2020

All Rights Reserved. No part of this book may be reproduced in any form without permission in writing from the author. Reviewers may quote brief passages in reviews.

Disclaimer: No part of this publication may be reproduced or transmitted in any form or by any means, mechanical or electronic, including photocopying or recording, or by any information storage and retrieval system, or transmitted by email without permission in writing from the publisher.

While all attempts have been made to verify the information provided in this publication, neither the author nor the publisher assumes any responsibility for errors, omissions or contrary interpretations of the subject matter herein.

This book is for entertainment purposes only. The views expressed are those of the author alone, and should not be taken as expert instruction or commands. The reader is responsible for his or her own actions.

Adherence to all applicable laws and regulations, including international, federal, state and local laws governing professional licensing, business practices, advertising and all other aspects of doing business in the US, Canada, UK or any other jurisdiction is the sole responsibility of the purchaser or reader.

Neither the author nor the publisher assumes any responsibility or liability whatsoever on the behalf of the purchaser or reader of these materials. Any perceived slight of any individual or organization is purely unintentional.

Free Bonus from Captivating History (Available for a Limited time)

Hi History Lovers!

Now you have a chance to join our exclusive history list so you can get your first history ebook for free as well as discounts and a potential to get more history books for free! Simply visit the link below to join.

Captivatinghistory.com/ebook

Also, make sure to follow us on Facebook, Twitter and Youtube by searching for Captivating History.

Contents

INTRODUCTION: AN AMERICAN SUCCESS STORY 1

CHAPTER 1 - THE GROWING PAINS OF TEDDY ROOSEVELT 4

CHAPTER 2 - TRIED, TESTED, AND STANDING FIRM 12

CHAPTER 3 - THE MARCH TOWARD WAR 23

CHAPTER 4 - TEDDY'S RETURN TO ELECTED OFFICE 32

CHAPTER 5 - A SQUARE DEAL FOR EVERY MAN 37

CHAPTER 6 - THE PANAMA CANAL AND A BID FOR REELECTION ... 43

CHAPTER 7 - TWO WEDDINGS AND A SECOND TERM 49

CHAPTER 8 - THE LEAD-UP TO A POLITICAL APOCALYPSE 58

CHAPTER 9 - TEDDY'S FINAL RUN AND HIS RIVER OF DOUBT 68

CHAPTER 10 - A WORLD WAR AND A WORRIED FATHER 77

CONCLUSION: TEDDY'S LASTING LEGACY 88

REFERENCES: 93

Introduction: An American Success Story

The Roosevelt family would become a political dynasty in the United States, spanning from the late 19th century to the middle of the 20th century. The Roosevelt presence in America can be traced all the way back to their trail-blazing ancestor, Claes Martenszen van Roosevelt, a Dutchman who came to the New World with high hopes in 1644. Like many of those early American stories, the life of this very first American Roosevelt was one that went from rags to riches.

Claes came to America with not much more than the shirt on his back, but in the ensuing years, he managed to generate considerable wealth. Teddy's ancestor set up shop in a nascent New York (it was actually called New Amsterdam in those days), where he set the foundation for his future family's wealth through a variety of enterprises that included banking, real estate, glass manufacturing, and sugar crops, among other things.

So it was that several generations later, by the time Teddy Roosevelt was born on October 27th, 1858, the Roosevelts were one of the most affluent families in America. Despite the fact that he was born into great wealth, Teddy's parents tried hard to make sure that their son didn't take his inheritance for granted. His father, Theodore

Senior, who was himself a wealthy businessman, made it a habit to make sure that his son Teddy realized how blessed they were.

Theodore Sr. led by example, becoming a frequent benefactor of various charities and organizations for the needy. For example, Teddy's father was a founding partner for the New York Orthopedic Hospital, as well as the "Children's Aid Society," which was created with the aim of bringing a better life to the city's youth. It was through these means that this son of wealth was first introduced to the world of the less fortunate.

But perhaps the greatest education Teddy received on the hardship of life came by way of his own faltering personal health. Since he was a child, Teddy had been afflicted with bouts of severe asthma. He would wake up in the middle of the night, feeling as though he was being suffocated. Gasping for air, the young Teddy would cry out for his parents for help. His dear old mom and dad would dutifully rush to the struggling child's side, but despite their best efforts, they didn't quite know how to ease his suffering.

Asthma is a condition in which the bronchial tubes in the lungs suddenly become inflamed and constrict, narrowing the airways so badly that those suffering from it cannot seem to get enough oxygen. Not much was known about the affliction in those days, but eventually, it would be determined that the best medicine for little Teddy's inflamed bronchial tubes was fresh air and exercise. This was an area of Teddy's life that he would lay claim to with great vigor.

In many ways, it was in pure defiance of his often-sickly constitution that Roosevelt began, from a young age, to push himself further and harder than his peers. For it was this sickly asthmatic that would one day become a legendary "Rough Rider," leading the charge in the Spanish-American War.

It was this occasionally gasping for breath Teddy that would eventually climb to the highest office in the land and have his own face carved into the side of Mount Rushmore. The story of Teddy Roosevelt is, in many ways, the story of America. Teddy never let difficult circumstances hold him back. On the contrary, he used hurdles of adversity as his own personal springboard to achieve ultimate success.

Chapter 1 – The Growing Pains of Teddy Roosevelt

Teddy Roosevelt grew into a lively and inquisitive adolescent despite the fact that intervening bouts of ill health would occasionally leave him bedridden. It was due to the unpredictability of his condition that he did not attend a standard public school but instead was tutored by private instructors, a curriculum which his own mother Martha would have a hand in as the young man grew up in the cozy confines of his family's upscale New York estate.

Besides his parents and his tutors, the other common faces in Teddy's early years were, of course, his siblings, which were made up of an elder sister named Anna (whose nickname was "Bamie"), a younger sister Corinne, and a younger brother Elliott. Perhaps telling of the nature of Teddy's precarious health, Elliott, even though he was younger, often took on the role of being a big brother to Teddy. Elliott was said to be very protective of the ailing Teddy, making sure to ease his suffering in any way he could.

During his long stretches of illness, Teddy would often turn to books as both a source of education as well as a source of comfort. He excelled in his studies early on, and although his father Theodore Sr. was proud of his progress, it was his dad who held the chief concern that Teddy was becoming too bookish. Or, as he informed his son at the time, "You have the mind but not the body, and without the help of the body, the mind cannot go as far as it should. You must make your body."

Teddy's father was basically telling him that all the book knowledge in the world would not do him a bit of good if he couldn't even get out of bed. It was simple but sound advice that Teddy would take to heart. When he was well enough, Teddy began lifting weights and doing other exercises meant to strengthen his physical form. This new fitness regimen seemed to do much more than all the other homemade remedies he had been subjected to, and he did initially see some improvement of his condition after engaging in this new routine.

But the real impetus that led Teddy to take charge of his physical condition would come as a consequence of a particularly bad incident of bullying that Teddy endured at the age of thirteen. The confrontation occurred on an occasion that had the young Teddy traveling alone to a summer resort the Roosevelts made use of. It was while he was in transit, in the back of a stagecoach and without the protection of his doting family, that a couple of fellow passengers, some mischievous youths close to Teddy's age, began to take full advantage of Teddy's timidity.

The youths began to pick on Teddy, with their taunts escalating until they were physically manhandling him. Teddy attempted to defend himself but found that he was not able to fend off their abuse. Frightened and humiliated, the dejected Teddy decided from that day forward that he would learn how to fight. In order to do so, he took up boxing. It was a sport that Teddy, despite his small size, seemed to take to quite well, and soon he was even engaging in competitive matches, eventually winning in the lightweight division. As a reward for his efforts, it is said that he received nothing more than a "cheap pewter mug." Despite its cheapness, however, Teddy was said to have clung to that trophy for the rest of his life as one of his most prized possessions. For him, that mug signified his transformation from a bullied victim to a powerful champion of his own destiny. From that day forward, competition was everything for Roosevelt. Life was a challenge, and he was determined to answer it as best he could.

And whether he was boxing or studying for his coursework in school, Teddy always tried to put his best foot forward. This was evidenced at the age of fourteen when during a family excursion to Egypt, Teddy went on an outright hunting safari, keeping a journal of all of his adventures. One of his entries read, "February 5th: Shot a sand chat and an Egyptian plover and got a bat."

These adventures would be just a brief precursor to a life filled with all manner of legendary exploits. But as a young man, as much as Teddy sought out the life of an adventurer, a good solid education was still viewed as the surest path to success. And in this area, Teddy was certainly no slacker. His home curriculum was so advanced, in fact, that he was able to attend Harvard at just eighteen years old.

Teddy adjusted well to life at Harvard, but while he was away, he would be dealt his first major tragedy in life. For it was in the spring of 1878, while he was at Harvard, that Teddy would receive the news that his father was deathly ill. His father, in fact, had an advanced form of stomach cancer, and in an effort to shield his son from worry, he kept his failing health a secret. As soon as Teddy received word of his father's deteriorating state, he immediately dropped everything and hopped on the next train headed for New York. But sadly enough, by the time he arrived, his father had already died. It was hard for Teddy to deal with the loss. It seemed that the only way he could deal with the grief was to slightly disconnect from it. In a pattern that would repeat throughout his life, Teddy fought off his mourning by plowing ahead and working hard.

And in the hallowed halls of Harvard academia, Teddy showed himself to be an ideal pupil. He was not only studious but also ceaselessly inquisitive. During his senior year, while he was a member of the Phi Beta Kappa, he began an extensive analysis of something that had interested him for quite a while, the naval battles of the War of 1812. All of these efforts would culminate into what would become the academic text known as *The Naval War of 1812*.

This text would be held as an authoritative work on the subject for many years to come, and it would even be of some use to his relative and fellow future president Franklin Delano Roosevelt when he served as the assistant secretary to the US Navy from 1913 to 1920. But Teddy wasn't all work and no play during his Harvard years, for it was during this time that he would come to make the acquaintance of a young woman by the name of Alice Lee.

Alice was from Boston, and at only seventeen years of age, she was already quite stunning to behold. And when Teddy Roosevelt first laid eyes on her in the fall of 1878, it was said to have been a clear-cut case of "love at first sight." The smitten Teddy tried everything he could to win her heart, although, initially, Alice did not always reciprocate his affection, a fact that Teddy himself was painfully aware of.

For example, at one Harvard gathering they both attended, Teddy pointed her out of the crowd to a friend of his and declared, "See that girl? I am going to marry her. She won't have me, but I am going to have her!" As grandiose as his declaration may have been, however, he was right. And soon after he staked this claim, he and Alice were indeed engaged to be married.

The two would officially become husband and wife after graduation, getting married in 1880. After getting married, Teddy and Alice would find a place of their own in New York, where Teddy began to study law at the nearby Columbia University Law School. The legal field could not hold Teddy's attention, however, and soon enough, instead of just studying the law, he desired to legislate the law and dropped out of Columbia altogether in favor of a career in politics.

New York, which was his family's own personal stomping grounds, was as good a place as any for Teddy to try his luck with elected office, but he quickly realized that he wouldn't be able to get his foot in the door unless he could get past the party bosses. In those days, these so-called bosses of local political parties ran the show. They decided who would run and, in many cases, who would win before any votes were ever cast at the ballot box.

Roosevelt was rather stunned at just how corrupt local politics were at the time and found the local "political machines" that sought to automatically determine outcomes in elections distasteful, to say the least. As Teddy described it at the time:

> When I began to make inquiries as to the whereabouts of the local Republican association, the men I knew best laughed at me, and told me that politics was not controlled by "gentlemen." They assured me that the men I met would be rough and brutal and unpleasant to deal with. I answered that if this were so it merely meant that the people I knew did not belong to the governing class.

In other words, Roosevelt figured that if it was a brutal business, it was simply because the parties were made up of too many brutes. He thought the best remedy to this unsightly affair would be for a new crop of political players such as himself to come to prominence. Like always, the adventurous Roosevelt was up for the challenge. Even if every door of the party bosses slammed in his face, he was more than ready to kick them down of his own volition.

It wasn't long, however, before the party bosses themselves began to take notice of Roosevelt. Rather than oppose him, it was determined that it was in their favor to use an articulate young man from an affluent New York family for their own ends. It was in this fashion that the local Republican Party ended up nominating Roosevelt to run for the New York State Assembly. Even with the backing of the party bosses, Roosevelt made it clear from the beginning that if he were indeed successful as a candidate, he would not make himself indebted to the political machine once he took office.

And after he successfully bested his Democrat opponent, and was duly elected on November 8th, 1881, he made good on his pledge. This was unequivocally demonstrated shortly after he came to office when he tried to get rid of a local judge, who was supported by the local party bosses, on charges of corruption. Many of the party lackeys who viewed toeing the corrupt party line as sacrosanct were quick to write Teddy off for his efforts. He had, after all, just bit the hand that fed him, and the party bosses were sure to retaliate.

But Teddy was a smarter politician than any of them realized, and instead of relying upon the party bosses, he attempted to curry favor with his constituents. Soon it was clear that Teddy was popular enough with the average voter that he could stand up to the corrupt party officials any day of the week. And rather than seeking to curtail Teddy, the party bosses were themselves at Teddy's mercy as he began his own mission to clean house in New York's legislature.

His grateful constituents paid him back for his efforts in political housekeeping by electing Teddy not just once but three times. Teddy was his usual self, highly opinionated, during his time as a New York lawmaker, and once he decided upon something, it was hard to change his mind. But there were occasions when he could be persuaded. On one notable occasion, for example, Teddy was presented with a bill to outlaw the cigar-making sweatshops that were rife in New York City. Initially, Teddy opposed the measure, thinking that the legislature had no business telling people how to make a living. Samuel Gompers, a labor leader who championed the bill, persisted in changing Teddy's mind and actually took Teddy on a tour of some of the rundown sections of the city where the product was being ceaselessly rolled out. Of this experience, Teddy would recall, "The tobacco was stowed about everywhere, alongside the foul bedding, and in a corner, there were scraps of food. The men, women, and children in this room worked all day and far on into the evening, and they slept and ate there."

They say that seeing is believing, and after bearing witness to this awful sight, Teddy was indeed convinced that no one should work under such dreadful conditions, even if they wanted to. He was essentially converted on the spot and became the chief proponent of the bill, finally convincing New York's governor, Grover Cleveland, to take action and approve a bipartisan measure that would outlaw the slovenly sweatshops for good.

Teddy was rapidly proving himself to be a quick study when it came to politics and the human condition, and it was during his third term in office that Roosevelt began to really come into his own. He was a successful politician, happily married, and had a child on the way. He was on the upswing, and for him, life couldn't have been better. But all of this was about to change in the spring of 1884 when Roosevelt was struck a double blow in the form of both his wife and his mother developing a devastating illness, one after the other.

His wife would be beset with severe complications after giving birth to their first child, Alice, while his mother rapidly deteriorated from a bout of typhoid fever. Incredibly enough, both his wife and his mother would end up passing away, each one dying just hours apart from the other.

Teddy rushed his way south by train from Albany, New York, to Manhattan, eager to get away from his work in the legislature and see his family. During the train ride, he received a telegram that informed him that his child had just been born. The telegram read, "You have a baby girl. Congratulations." This telegram was then quickly followed by one that was not quite as celebratory in nature. It read, "Come at once. Mother and Alice gravely ill." Upon his arrival at the Roosevelt residence in Manhattan, Roosevelt found his wife Alice barely clinging to life. Her kidneys were failing her, resulting in bloody urine, back pain, and a sky-rocketing fever.

It is said that upon seeing her condition, he literally fell to his knees as he reached over the bed to put his arms around her one last time. But even as he held onto his dying wife, he heard his brother Elliott calling to him from the other room. "Teddy! Come at once if you want to see mother one last time!" In this house of terrible sadness that Teddy had stumbled into, it was not only his wife who was breathing her last but also his dear mother.

In a separate room, he found his mother in bed, delirious with typhoid fever and breathing her last breath. She would pass away first, leaving Teddy barely able to process the loss of his mother before frantically running back to the bedside of his dying wife. Clinging to Alice's failing form, he begged and pleaded with her to stay alive, but all to no avail. She, too, would pass a short time later.

One can only imagine the heartache and devastation Teddy must have felt to return home only to be greeted with the deaths of both of his most beloved family members. Teddy's journal entry from the time perhaps sums up the sentiment best, as he wrote, "For joy or for sorrow, my life has now been lived out." He felt as though his entire life had already run its course, leaving him all alone to pick up the pieces.

But as much as Teddy wished to curl up into a ball of despair, his fighting spirit would eventually rise to the surface once more. As Teddy would later recall, "It was a grim and evil fate, but I have never believed it did any good to flinch or yield for any blow, nor does it lighten the blow to cease from working." Teddy, despite his despair, charged forward and buried himself in his work.

Teddy couldn't face the terrible pain he felt. With the deaths of his mother and wife, the roles of husband and son had been ripped away from him, and under the circumstances, the role of being a father was something that he could barely even fathom. So it was that all he had left at the moment was to return to his role as an assemblyman in New York's state capital of Albany, while his daughter Alice was left in the loving care of Teddy's sister Bamie.

Turning his face from his personal life completely, Teddy plunged himself into his profession. During this term in office, he would busy himself with investigations into corruption, attend countless hearings, and submit several bills aimed at reform. During this time of personal crisis, he found it most expedient to take on the mantle of a champion of the people. Rather than dwelling on his own sorrow, Teddy took on the malpractice of corporate monopolies, which was incredibly rife in the country at the time. Here, Teddy's corruption-busting bravado could serve as a convenient cover for his own personal anguish and devastation.

Chapter 2 – Tried, Tested, and Standing Firm

In 1884, America was once again knee-deep in a presidential election year. Just prior to the Republican National Convention, Teddy had supported an up and coming Republican by the name of George F. Edmunds instead of the favored candidate, Senator James G. Blaine. Although Senator Blaine wasn't Teddy's first choice, when the die was cast, and it was clear that he would be the Republican nominee, Roosevelt made it a point to get behind the man who would be the chosen Republican candidate.

Even though he managed to best his rivals in the party, Blaine came into the general election as a damaged candidate with corruption and scandal swirling around his campaign. Blaine was also against the reformative measures of government that Teddy Roosevelt very much stood for at the time. Having said that, it came as a surprise to many of Teddy's contemporaries that he would stump for a candidate who was so at odds with his own opinions.

Teddy saw it differently, however, and even though some of his peers jumped ship and went so far as to even support the Democrat candidate, Grover Cleveland, Teddy stayed loyal to his party, stating that he was "duty bound to support the choice of the majority." He gained some esteem from his colleagues as a man dedicated to his political party, but at the same time, he developed considerable friction with personal friends who considered a Blaine candidacy abhorrent.

They did not need to worry too much about that because, in the end, Grover Cleveland defeated Blaine and became the next president. In the aftermath of this contentious election, Teddy felt that it was time for him to take a break and temporarily get away from New York's political racket. Leaving his children in the care of relatives, he set off to a piece of land in North Dakota he had just purchased in order to try his luck as a ranch hand.

Known as the "Badlands," this remote piece of North Dakota Territory was indeed part of America's still wild and untamed West. North Dakota was not even a state at the time, as it didn't enter the Union until 1889. It was just the kind of place that Teddy could use to unwind and vent his pent-up anxiety by physically exerting himself on the range. Just as was the case when he was a child suffering from asthma, Teddy found that the best release available to him was through hands-on adventures in the great outdoors.

Leaving the trappings of the New York high life behind, Teddy wanted to eke out an existence on the open frontier just like the rough and ready local ranch hands who worked on the property. But all the local ranchers had to do was take one look at Teddy to determine that he was out of place. Along with his New York accent, his idea of ranch attire was decidedly different from the usual cowboys that inhabited the range. It is said that Teddy wore a large "sombrero type hat" along with "an elaborately fringed and beaded leather shirt" that immediately marked him out as an out-of-touch city slicker. He was also widely ridiculed over the glasses he wore to cure his nearsightedness—a feature that regularly brought forth the mocking moniker of "four eyes" from the rugged ranch hands when referring to Teddy. The fact that Teddy didn't drink or smoke was a problem as well, with many of the regulars taking it for a sign of softness. But Teddy Roosevelt would prove his mettle soon enough.

The defining moment came when he stepped into a bar after a long day of work and sat down for a drink. As soon as one of the local tough guys saw him, the man drunkenly shouted, "Four Eyes is going to treat!" In other words, he was proclaiming that the soft outsider with his distinctive clothes and glasses was going to be pressured into buying the whole saloon a round of drinks. Teddy ignored the drunk, however, and continued about his business as if he didn't hear him. Thinking that he had found a meek and mild target, the drunk continued his harassment, walking right up to Teddy and once again proclaiming that Teddy was going to open his wallet and buy everybody a bottle of booze. In response to this provocation, Teddy turned around and replied in a quiet, measured tone, "If I've got to. I've got to." The intoxicated troublemaker must have been grinning with glee, assuming that he had just successfully bullied the stranger into buying a round of drinks.

But Teddy's words were not so much in answer to his demands, as they were in reference to Teddy's own internal thought process over whether or not to knock the creep out. Realizing he had no other choice, Teddy took one look at the jerk, shrugged, then muttered, "If I've got to. I've got to," before jumping out of his seat and punching the man with full force right in the face. Lying unconscious on the floor, this debauched local did not bother anyone else for the rest of the night.

By then, Teddy's associates on the range were certainly singing a different tune, with one of his ranch hands later making the remark, "That four-eyed maverick has got sand in his craw aplenty. He's sure a man to hold up his end." Soon enough, the "four-eyed maverick" from New York was a regular fixture on the ranch. He even managed to put some of his previous legislative experience to use by way of becoming a chairman of the "Little Missouri River Stockmen's Association," which was a regional arbiter for ranchers in those days. It was an organization designed to look out for ranchers and make sure that they weren't taken advantage of by their neighbors. The official charter for the group actually read in part, "The object of this association is to advance the interests of stock-growers and dealers in livestock of all kinds in Western Dakota, and for the purpose of the protection of the same against frauds and swindlers."

The sentiment was very much in line with Teddy's corruption-busting past in the legislature, and as chairman, he was just as determined to keep ranching protocol on the up and up as he was when it came to New York business practices. Along with this, Teddy was also a hands-on leader on the range, spending several days on end in the saddle. On one occasion, he even rode all night long in the pouring rain just to rescue a pack of cattle that had taken flight after being spooked by thunder and lightning.

When Roosevelt wasn't riding the range, he was quite a prolific writer, compiling a historical piece on the Wild West, as well as penning a biography on a little-known senator from Missouri named Thomas Hart Benton, who had lived some one hundred years before. But Teddy's greatest pastime was always hunting. Teddy loved to hunt, enjoying the buildup just as much as the actual hunting itself.

During these legendary excursions, Teddy encountered everything from bears, mountain goats, and even an aggressive band of Native Americans, who he claimed he had to "drive off with his rifle" in order to save his own life. Of course, it must be noted that on many of these occasions, Teddy had no other witnesses except for his own conscience. So, for much of these tales, we have to depend upon the veracity of his personal version of events and nothing else.

At any rate, the accounts he put down were riveting all the same. For example, on the occasion that he allegedly faced down a bear and lived to tell the tale, he reported the following:

> Cocking my rifle and stepping quickly forward I found myself face to face with the great bear, who was less than twenty-five feet off. At that distance and in such a place it was very necessary to kill or disable him at the first fire; doubtless my face was pretty white, but the blue barrel was steady as a rock as I glanced along it until I could see the top of the head fairly between his two sinister looking eyes.

That must have been a frightening sight, to say the least. Teddy then goes on to state, "As I pulled the trigger I jumped aside out of the smoke, to be ready if he charged, but it was needless, for the great brute was struggling in the death agony. The bullet hole in his skull was exactly between his eyes. This bear was nearly nine feet long and weighed over a thousand pounds."

However, by late 1886, Roosevelt was finally growing weary of his solitary life on the range and returned to his old stomping grounds of New York. It was upon his return that he began to go on frequent outings with a certain Ms. Edith Kermit Carow. Teddy had actually known Edith since childhood, and the two were highly compatible and seemed to like each other a great deal. But Teddy Roosevelt, as well as some of his family members, was concerned that he was moving on too quickly by marrying so soon after the death of his first wife.

His sisters Bamie and Corinne, in particular, also seemed to disapprove of the match, speaking directly to Teddy about their misgivings. Edith had been a childhood acquaintance of Corine's, and the idea that Teddy would marry someone that she had known so intimately in the past was aggravating for a wide variety of reasons. She is said to have found the news of their engagement "all too incomprehensible."

While his family was becoming increasingly uncomfortable with his courtship of Edith, Teddy decided to try his luck once again with local politics. In the fall of 1886, Teddy threw his hat into the New York City mayoral race. It proved to be an uphill battle, however, since his opponent from the Democrat Party, Abram Hewitt, was a decided favorite. In the end, Roosevelt's campaign tanked on election day, receiving just 27 percent of the votes.

With his hopes for mayor dashed, Teddy Roosevelt decided it was time to make good on his intent to marry Edith. And despite the displeasure of some of his family members with the union, the two were duly wed on December 28th, 1886. With Edith, Teddy would eventually have five more children, in addition to Teddy's daughter from his previous marriage, Alice.

In the spring of 1887, Teddy and his new wife moved into a home in New York's Oyster Bay area. It was a sprawling 22-room mansion that Teddy had begun construction on a few years prior. After his first wife's abrupt passing, the home remained vacant. It wasn't until after his marriage to Edith that Teddy was ready to finally settle into the property. Later known as "Sagamore Hill," this estate would come to serve not only as a place for Teddy to raise his family but also as a meeting house for important political discourse.

Edith would give birth to the new couple's first son that fall. The child was named Theodore, like his father, and for much of his life, he would be known as Theodore Jr. or simply just Ted. Teddy Roosevelt, meanwhile, was completely overjoyed. Perfectly happy and content with his new house, new wife, and new son, he declared, "I am very glad our house has an heir at last!"

Teddy spent the next few months mostly around Sagamore Hill, writing and spending time with his family. He had thought that he had left politics behind, but soon enough, his eyes began to look toward the upcoming 1888 Republican National Convention. Benjamin Harrison, whose grandfather was former President William Henry Harrison, proved to have the name recognition necessary to gain the nomination of the party.

Roosevelt, eager to get back into the thick of politics, vigorously stumped for the candidate. It was due to his enthusiastic support that Teddy was tapped for a role in Harrison's administration after Harrison was elected. President Benjamin Harrison placed Teddy on the United States Civil Service Commission. This was a special oversight committee that had been created in order to combat the so-called "spoils system," which had become so endemic in politics at the time.

The term "spoils system" was in reference to the concept that once a candidate was victorious in a political campaign, they developed a "to the victor goes the spoils" sort of attitude when it came to who they appointed to serve in their administration. In other words, it had become quite customary for politicians who had just won an election to hand out political spoils in the form of special appointments in government and seats on powerful boards that they otherwise would have had no business being on.

The critics of this habit charged that good and able-bodied government employees were often displaced after an election so an incoming administration could put their own people in place. They stated that those who were inserted in the place of the original employees were often not as experienced or equipped for the job as their political predecessors were. Teddy, who had always been a critic of the practice, got back to his reformer roots, as he sought to weed out the corrupt cronyism that was in place.

It was an uphill battle, and Roosevelt's resources for the task at hand were quite limited, but he found that by galvanizing the news media to the plight, he could get more accomplished than he otherwise would. Long before the era of reality TV, Teddy proved that he was a larger-than-life personality, as he was able to garner attention with grandiose statements and the sheer force of his personality.

Chastising those who would attempt to give away positions solely as a political favor, Teddy made sure that all qualifying civil service tests were taken by those entering new positions to ensure that any new candidates were actually able to do the jobs that they were placed in. He also created several revisions of civil service examinations that were already on the books in order to make sure that they remained relevant to the positions that were being applied for. This can be seen when Teddy updated the civil exam for becoming a border guard to include examinations revolving around one's ability to handle a gun and ride the range, two valuable skills that were needed for any would-be border agent. Roosevelt was quite serious about his role in the Civil Service Commission. So much so that he didn't even hesitate to go against his own party and criticize the sitting Republican president,

Benjamin Harrison, for what he charged to be "kowtowing" to the demands of the spoils system.

Things then came to a head in 1891 when Teddy challenged Postmaster General John Wanamaker's decision to clean house and get rid of a large number of employees at the post office in favor of his own appointments, which was in direct violation of the civil service law. An investigation ensued, and Harrison and Wanamaker were both found to be in the wrong. Wanamaker, as it turned out, had been a great financial contributor to President Harrison's campaign.

Harrison was, of course, duly enraged by the developments, but Teddy had become so ingratiated in the press as a corruption fighter that Harrison didn't dare fire him. Teddy, working out of the same playbook he used against local party bosses when he served as an assemblyman in Albany, was able to gird himself with just enough public support to ensure that he was untouchable.

And following President Harrison's ultimate defeat in the 1892 election to Grover Cleveland, Teddy was so universally trusted and popular that he got to keep his job. The incoming Democrat president opted to keep Teddy right where he was. In the meantime, Teddy's family back on Sagamore Hill was steadily growing with the birth of his second son, Kermit, in the fall of 1889 and a daughter named Ethel in the summer of 1891.

As much joy as Teddy's growing family was bringing him, the growing family and untoward peccadilloes of his brother Elliott were also driving him mad. Elliott, who had begun life with much promise, had since devolved into a life of drunken debauchery. He had married a New York socialite by the name of Anna Hall, with whom he would have three children.

But it was a child that he allegedly conceived with a former household servant named Catherine "Katy" Mann that would send the family into an uproar. Mann ended up blackmailing the family, demanding some ten thousand dollars to keep quiet about the matter. Although it was his brother Elliott's infidelity that had created the drama, Teddy, ever sensitive about his image, was not willing to let even his brother's indiscretion besmirch his pristine reputation.

As such, the family ended up agreeing to buy Katy's silence. The child she birthed meanwhile, Elliott Roosevelt Mann, would live in relative obscurity, with only a few key members of the family knowing the secret. After this debacle came to a close, Teddy's relationship with his brother went from bad to worse. Increasingly alarmed at his brother's habits, Teddy began to take a more authoritarian role over his brother's life.

These efforts would culminate with Teddy attempting to have his troubled sibling declared incompetent as a last-ditch effort to prevent him from squandering the family's wealth and generating even more scandal. Teddy, however, soon realized that the mere effort of doing so would generate the very public scrutiny that he wished to avoid and decided to forego this option. Instead, Teddy confronted his brother directly, and after a stern heart to heart, he had Elliott personally agree to all of his terms.

Teddy demanded that Elliott enter into a rehabilitation program and separate from his wife Anna until he had substantially recovered. It sounds rather incredible that Teddy would force his brother to leave his own wife, but this is what happened. Teddy knew that his brother was in no state to serve as the head of his own household, and he feared that the drunken and irresponsible Elliott would simply make more babies, thereby multiplying his problems, if he remained under the same roof as his spouse. While Elliott did not actually divorce his wife, it was agreed that they would remain separated until Elliott was able to make a full recovery.

Once in rehab, Elliott initially made good progress and seemed to be on the verge of reclaiming his life. But right when he was near recovery, an unforeseen and especially cruel tragedy would strike. In December 1892, his wife Anna would contract diphtheria and abruptly pass away. The major incentive for Elliott to get clean was so he could reunite with his wife. With this taken away from him, he soon relapsed right back into his old drinking habits.

And if things weren't bad enough, the following year, his son Elliott Jr. suddenly died as well. Elliott would remain in an inconsolable, drunken stupor for the rest of 1893 and much of 1894, which was the year he died. After repeated drinking binges, Elliott had become more and more unstable until he was at the point of having delirious hallucinations. He eventually died, thrashing and writhing, the victim of an apparent seizure, in August 1894. Teddy had a horrible time coming to grips with the tragedy, and his sister Corinne would later recall that Teddy "cried like a child" in the days after his passing. Nevertheless, Teddy was also partially relieved to know that his brother's suffering was finally over.

In the midst of all of this tragedy and turmoil, Teddy Roosevelt was steadily gaining recognition as a rising star of the Republican Party. His work on the Civil Service Commission had brought him much of this esteem, but by 1895, Teddy would ultimately decide to resign in favor of a new line of work. For it was at this time that Teddy had decided to put aside his role on the commission in order to even more directly challenge abuse and corruption by becoming the police commissioner of New York City.

The NYPD most certainly was corrupt in those days, with nepotism and even financial bribes often serving as the lubrication for promotion. Crooked cops also often worked in tandem with crime bosses, choosing to ignore criminal enterprises if the price or politics were right. Teddy arrived on the scene as commissioner in May of 1895, and he immediately set out to change the status quo.

In his first week alone, Teddy had managed to terminate Superintendent Tom Byrnes, and he stood ready to get rid of anyone else that might be a hindrance to the fair and equal rule of the law. But perhaps most importantly, Teddy was a hands-on figure who took it upon himself to walk the beats that local cops patrolled, directly critiquing their actions and calling out corruption when he saw it. Teddy had declared that it was *his duty* "to make matters very unpleasant for policemen who shirk *their duty*."

And true to his word, he didn't hesitate to pull drunk cops out of bars and call out idle police loitering in back alleys or even sleeping on the job to work harder. The press, meanwhile, absolutely ate it up, and once again, Teddy Roosevelt had become something akin to a media darling. He was known as the corruption-busting police commissioner who actually took an active role in his job and personally patrolled the streets of New York.

As one writer for the newspaper, the *New York World*, declared at the time, "We have a real Police Commissioner. His teeth are big and white, his eyes are small and piercing, his voice rasping. His heart is full of reform, and a policeman in full uniform, with helmet, revolver and night stick is no more to him than a plain, every-day human being."

In other words, the citizens of New York, which was more likely to fear the police than turn to them for help, was beginning to see a true leader stand up to the corruption that had been so endemic in the ranks of the NYPD. After either getting rid of or just severely chastising these bad apples, Teddy revitalized the police department, making it once again efficient and accountable to the public that they were there to serve.

Along with these measures of reform, Teddy was also instrumental in modernizing police equipment. It was Teddy Roosevelt who oversaw the implementation of a brand-new telephone system for the NYPD.

As usual, Teddy was a man for all seasons. Whether riding the wild range of the West or walking the equally wild streets of New York, Teddy strictly stuck to his personal convictions—and his actions clearly proved it.

Chapter 3 – The March toward War

As successful as Roosevelt was as a police commissioner, by the time of the 1896 presidential election, he was beginning to grow weary of his post. He had succeeded well enough, but toward the end of his tenure, Teddy had encountered something he had not quite anticipated: stern opposition from the public. His trouble began when he led a campaign against the so-called "Sunday Saloons."

In New York, there was a state law that forbade the selling of alcohol on Sundays. Although this law was on the books, it was constantly being violated by bars and pubs that were willing to look the other way. These were the infamous Sunday Saloons, which were supposed to be closed but would leave their backdoor open on Sundays so that thirsty patrons could step right in for a drink. Teddy himself was not so much against the fact that people wanted to have a drink as he was that doing so on a Sunday was against the law.

Furthermore, those who violated the statute invited all manner of corruption into practice. Saloons that were in good standing with the police department, and perhaps paid a bribe or two, were able to get by with staying open on a Sunday. An establishment that was not in with the police in such a manner just might get raided. It was this endemic corruption, which resulted from the sordid situation, that concerned Teddy the most.

In order to stem the flow of corruption, Teddy ordered a wholesale shutdown of all liquor-selling establishments on Sundays. The public outrage at this act was immense, however, and soon legislators up for reelection were seeking to find ways to ameliorate the common man's displeasure. They created a legal loophole by passing a bill that enabled hotels to sell alcohol with meals on Sunday.

It seemed reasonable enough at the time, but all things have consequences. And it wasn't long before crafty liquor vendors were attempting to take full advantage of it. Suddenly, there were alcohol-selling establishments popping up on every corner claiming to be a hotel when, in reality, they weren't. At this point, Roosevelt grew weary of his efforts and began to once again consider politics as his way out.

His opportunity came when the Republican presidential candidate, William McKinley, successfully won the 1896 election that November, opening the door for Roosevelt to get a position with the new administration. Recognizing Teddy Roosevelt's unique talents, McKinley tapped him for the role of assistant secretary of the navy.

Teddy, who had written the classic text, *The Naval War of 1812*, was already an expert in the field and seemed tailor-made for the role. And just in time. The US Navy had become somewhat diminished in previous administrations, but by the time of President McKinley, this branch of the US military was on a decided upswing, and Teddy was determined to make sure that this renaissance continued.

Taking office as assistant secretary in the spring of 1897, Teddy Roosevelt was determined to take the helm with gusto. He was eager to build up the military, and if the navy ended up butting heads with any foreign powers in the process, Roosevelt was ready for action. Some, in fact, would say that he welcomed it. This was evidenced in correspondence Roosevelt carried out with one of his friends later that year, in which he confessed, "In strict confidence, I should welcome any war. The country needs one."

Today, such sentiment would be rather shocking and appear to embody all of the trappings of what one might call a warmonger. Yet Teddy saw it differently; from his perspective, he felt that the United States had become complacent and stagnant during peacetime, and he couldn't help but feel that a war would shake things up enough to reinvigorate the nation.

As soon as he was signed on as assistant secretary, Teddy didn't waste any time getting the nation on track for potential future conflicts. In these efforts, he applied his typical hands-on approach and was soon personally touring battleships and inspecting the readiness of personnel. Teddy, the ultimate reformer, now made it his duty to root out unnecessary bureaucracy in the US Navy, streamlining protocol and urging the recruitment of the most talented officers.

He also sent urgent requests for the building of more ships, although many didn't see the necessity of such a thing at the time. Although Teddy was just the assistant secretary, the relaxed attitude of his immediate overseer, the actual secretary of the navy, John D. Long, allowed Teddy to have relatively free reign. And he made use of it. Among other things, Teddy frequently notified McKinley of his opinions on battleships that needed to be scrapped and on ships that needed to have some upgrades.

Teddy seemed to be building up the navy for an imminent showdown—but with who? Besides domestic conflicts with Native American tribes in the West, the United States had basically enjoyed an era of peace after the end of the Civil War. Teddy's wartime readiness would soon prove to be quite prescient, however, as a new political atmosphere began to take shape some three hundred miles from the southern tip of Florida in what was then Spanish-controlled Cuba.

Cuba had long been a possession of Spain, but a revolution was now rocking the island. These rumblings for independence did not begin overnight, as the island had a long history of rebellions dating back decades before. Most significantly was Spain's emancipation of former slaves on the island in 1886, which led to not only a change in the status quo but also a dramatic shift in the economy.

Ever since its colonization by Spain in the 1500s, the island of Cuba had been used as one massive sugar cane plantation, with slaves working the fields. With the end of slavery, previously wealthy Cuban plantation owners were often forced to close up shop, and many left their plantations altogether. This all had a ripple effect on the Cuban economy, and the dissatisfied Cubans began to openly rebel against Spanish control of the island.

While these efforts at independence were building in Cuba, Spain began to also have uprisings in its other far-flung colony—the Philippines. Now facing problems from territories in two different oceans, an already strained Spain found itself having to suppress both Cuban rebels in the Atlantic and Filipino agitators in the Pacific. A growing community of Cuban exiles who had taken refuge in Florida had been spreading the word of the latest happenings of the conflict to America.

There were indeed those who wished to aid the Cubans, but others were a bit more cautious in their sentiment. However, Teddy Roosevelt was not one of them, and as newspaper headlines began to proclaim Spain's ill treatment of Cuban civilians, Teddy was itching for a fight. In his own words, Teddy stated on record that he could not "understand how the bulk of the people can tolerate the hideous infamy that has attended the last two years of Spanish rule in Cuba. The time has come for us to fight."

President McKinley, on the other hand, had a more cautious mindset, and he had, up until that point, carefully avoided getting entangled in a war with Spain. Nevertheless, Teddy was actively preparing for war all the same, even if it meant taking action behind the backs of his superiors. In fact, in early 1898, when Secretary of the US Navy John D. Long was away on other business, Teddy Roosevelt took the opportunity to contact Commodore George Dewey, who oversaw the US fleet that was situated around Hong Kong. Teddy informed Dewey to "Keep full coal. In the event of war—see that the

Spanish squadron does not leave the Asiatic coast and then [begin] offensive operations in Philippine Islands." Teddy had basically outlined his planned offensive against the Spanish. He knew that in the event of war with Spain, the Philippines would need to be secured in order to prevent Spanish reinforcements from coming to Cuba. When Long heard of what Teddy had done, he was infuriated, but after giving it some thought, he decided not to refute the instructions.

This would prove to be a wise decision, for when war broke out that spring, Teddy's plan of action proved to be the best methodology for American intervention in Cuba. The spark that actually ignited the Spanish-American War occurred on February 15th, 1898, when an American warship, the USS *Maine*, which had been dispatched to Havana on the grounds of "protecting" American diplomats, was blown to smithereens.

Along with the complete destruction of the craft, it is said that a little over 260 Americans lost their lives. To this day, the cause of the sinking of the *Maine* has been disputed. At the time, many were quick to say that it was caused by the external explosion of a mine, thereby laying the blame at the feet of Spain. In later years, however, it has been argued that the detonation of the *Maine* could have been accidentally caused by magazines on board the vessel being "ignited by a spontaneous fire in a coal bunker."

Whatever the case may be, soon after America received this stunning blow, the war-ready Roosevelt was finally obliged with the war he had long sought. And as tensions reached a boiling point, the United States officially declared war on Spain on April 25th, 1898. As the hostilities commenced, Teddy's directive more or less went as planned. After the war was declared, Commodore Dewey was given the go-ahead and sped right over to the Philippines, where he proceeded to make short work of the outdated Spanish armada that was stationed there.

This meant that Spanish reinforcements wouldn't be readily available to help out in Cuba, thereby giving the green light for American troops to make landfall on the island. Incredibly enough, once the invasion was imminent, Teddy didn't hesitate to sign up. To the shock and disbelief of his peers, Teddy was completely willing to give up his prestigious post so that he could render his services right in the thick of combat.

Even though President McKinley himself had asked Teddy to remain stateside during the engagement, he couldn't resist. Furthermore, he wished to let everyone know that he was a man who practiced what he preached. Or, as he himself described it, "I have consistently preached the doctrine of a resolute foreign policy and of readiness to accept the arbitrament of the sword if necessary. Now the occasion has arisen, and I ought to meet it."

The person who was most distressed at Teddy's departure was, of course, his wife Edith, who by that time had birthed an additional two children: Archibald in 1894 and their youngest and final child, Quentin, in 1897. Edith was being left behind with this full house of youngsters while her husband put his life at risk. The fear and apprehension she felt was tremendous, but she put on a brave face nonetheless.

It was on May 6th, 1898, that Teddy took the unprecedented step of putting in his resignation as assistant secretary of the US Navy. With his resignation in order, he then went about cobbling together his own "volunteer cavalry regiment." This band of brothers would come to comprise one of the most diverse fighting regiments of its day. It had young ranch hands from the West, as well as cops Teddy had worked with on the East Coast. It was also a diverse bunch ethnically speaking, with Native Americans, African Americans, and Hispanics readily filling up the ranks.

As enthusiastic as Teddy was for the expedition, he himself had never actually served in the military in any official capacity as a field commander. As such, Teddy allowed his group to be under the direct supervision of a veteran officer named Colonel Leonard Wood, while Teddy accepted a commission under Wood as a "lieutenant colonel." Before Teddy and his men ever reached Cuba, they made a pitstop in San Antonio, Texas, for training.

Here, the wild bunch of recruits proved to be a bit too spirited for the locals, as their energy was spent mostly on drinking and causing mischief at local hangouts. Teddy, at one point, attempted to chastise them, but these efforts were immediately negated after one fine day of training when an obliging Teddy found it fit to indulge his troops. After several hours of drilling, Teddy sought to reward the dedicated recruits by taking them to a local establishment and announcing, "The men can go in and drink all the beer they want, which I will pay for!"

Many Texans probably breathed a collective sigh of relief when the rowdy bunch was transferred to Tampa, Florida, to await their final transport to Cuba. At any rate, the troops and the average citizens both survived the rambunctious weeks during which the new cadets trained, and the so-called Rough Riders finally made their way to Cuba on June 22nd, 1898, where they made landfall off the shores of the town of Daiquirí, some fourteen miles to the east of Santiago de Cuba. The irony of these "Rough Riders" is that, with the exception of Teddy, they didn't actually ride into battle on horses. Due to the cramped quarters of their landing craft, only officers like Teddy were allowed the luxury of bringing horses with them.

The initial plan involved the seizure of this strategically important port city. This would be done by sending the US ground forces, along with Cuban revolutionaries, into Santiago, while the US Navy fought off Spanish warships in the waters surrounding the port. Moving toward Santiago, Teddy and his men first encountered resistance near the region of Las Guásimas, where they were waylaid by the Spanish, resulting in a loss of sixteen men.

In the end, Teddy and his troops were victorious, and they managed to secure an important mountain pass for their efforts. It was around this time that Colonel Leonard Wood was promoted to brigadier general. Teddy would then get his own promotion on June 30th, making him an all-out colonel. So it was that Colonel Teddy Roosevelt and his men made their way to the San Juan highlands, located just outside of Santiago, on July 1st, where they engaged the enemy at a spot called "Kettle Hill."

The hillside was supposedly named as such because a large sugar refining kettle was on top of it. According to Teddy's later recollection, the fight for Kettle Hill commenced after he "waved his hat." With this signal, Teddy's band charged up the hill and opened up on the Spanish, who immediately returned fire in kind. Teddy himself was grazed by a bullet, and he quite possibly avoided imminent death by enacting a quick evasive maneuver that left a Spanish officer dead in his wake.

As the Spanish troops began to retreat, Teddy then rallied his men to charge after them up a nearby hilltop, leading to what would become the infamous "Battle of San Juan Hill." With a "take no prisoners" kind of mentality, the Rough Riders overwhelmed the Spanish defenders and forced them to flee. Pushed back into Santiago, the Spanish troops, which were under the direction of one Admiral Pascual Cervera, attempted to board Spanish ships parked in the harbor. But there was no easy way out for them since, following Teddy's previous directive, the US Navy was already in place to intercept them.

As soon as the ships left port, the waiting American warships let loose with a blistering bombardment that blasted the Spanish craft to pieces, resulting in the death of over 300 men, as well as some 1,700 being taken as prisoner. The Spanish fleet was destroyed, but there were still Spanish ground forces holed up in Santiago. The city was ultimately placed under siege for two weeks until this last holdout was finally convinced to surrender.

Soon thereafter, the Spanish had no choice but to sue for peace with preliminary talks beginning that August, with the terms being finalized on December 10th, 1898. This spelled the end for the Spanish Empire, with Spain handing over Puerto Rico, Guam, and the Philippines to the United States, along with temporarily making Cuba a US protectorate while the Cubans hammered out the terms of their independence.

Teddy and his Rough Riders, meanwhile, had already returned home that summer. Their first point of arrival was at a base on

"Montauk Point" in Long Island, New York. Here they were placed under quarantine for a short time to make sure that none of them had contracted the dreaded yellow fever that had been running rampant in the tropics. In the end, more of Teddy's men had indeed died from disease than from battle.

After a few weeks of observation, they were then given the green light to return stateside. Teddy and his men would go their separate ways, but Teddy would always look back proudly at their efforts, and when possible, he would even try to find positions for some of his former associates. Teddy himself would receive a new line of work when he was nominated by the Republican Party as the governor of New York.

Chapter 4 – Teddy's Return to Elected Office

At the time of New York's 1898 gubernatorial election, the Republicans had already had an incumbent in office, but the current Republican governor, Frank S. Black, was so unpopular that the party was desperately looking for another more palatable candidate to give the nomination to. The local party boss, New York Senator Thomas Platt, considered Teddy as a good candidate due to the high level of popularity he had achieved during his exploits with the Rough Riders in the Spanish-American War.

Platt was a little bit skeptical of whether or not Teddy would be a reliable team player for the party, but he knew that Teddy was the strongest candidate that they would be able to muster for the 1898 gubernatorial election. Teddy was indeed able to take the nomination away from the incumbent Republican governor and then went on to beat his Democrat opponent, Augustus Van Wyck, in the general election.

Roosevelt, his wife, and all six of his children would spend the next few years living in the governor's mansion, although it had actually been suggested that his eldest child, and the only one from his previous marriage, Alice, might attend a boarding school instead.

Alice did not like the notion one bit, however, and made her displeasure quite clear.

It is said that when she found out about the plans to ship her off to boarding school, she bluntly issued the warning, "If you send me, I will humiliate you. I will do something that will shame you. I tell you I will." Alice had grown into a headstrong young woman, and her family apparently took her by her word. And soon thereafter, they let the matter quietly drop.

Family drama aside, upon becoming governor, Roosevelt made sure that everything he did was in perfect harmony with the duties of his office. He arrived on time every day and utilized a highly regimented form of time management, in which crucial aspects of his workday, such as replying to correspondence, holding conferences with staff, and speaking with the press, were all accounted for.

During his first few months in office, Roosevelt's primary efforts involved battling corruption and invigorating New York's economy. This meant that Teddy was knee-deep in matters concerning corporate reform and labor unions. One of his most consequential bills while in office was the "Ford Franchise Tax Bill." This bit of legislation served to ensure that corporate-controlled public franchises paid their proper dues when it came to taxes.

But even though his job as governor had him mostly looking inward to domestic issues, it wasn't long before Roosevelt became concerned with matters on the national stage. The aftermath of the Spanish-American War, which he had championed and taken such a leading role in, was still unfolding. And although the war had been a stunning success in sheer military terms, by 1899, there was much argument as to just what should happen to America's new far-flung territorial possessions.

The most polarizing of these acquisitions was the Philippines. Located several thousand miles away in the middle of the Pacific Ocean, the Philippines were the most remote of the territorial gains. It was also the most culturally different, with a very different history—

more distant than even Cuba and Puerto Rico, at least as it pertained to the American experience.

Many felt that the US had no business in the Philippines and decried it as abject colonialism or even imperialism. Indeed, the most bellicose of critics even lambasted President William McKinley for attempting to create an American empire at the expense of the Filipinos. It was, for a wide variety of reasons, that detractors criticized the push to annex the Philippines to the United States.

But no doubt the most powerful argument came from those who brought up the interests of the Filipinos themselves, suggesting that they did not ask or want American intervention in their lives. The Filipinos, after all, had been rebelling against Spain's colonial grip for decades. Why then would they want America to simply take Spain's place at the helm?

Teddy, of course, saw things differently, and he refused to entertain the notion that the United States should give up such a hard-won piece of real estate as the Philippines. Or, as Teddy himself had declared at the time, "It now rests with our statesmen to see that the triumph is not made void." Roosevelt stressed that the American lives lost in securing the Philippines should not be wasted, and he wanted to do everything he could to ensure that this wouldn't be the case.

As governor of New York, however, entangled in day-to-day politics in the state, there was little he could do other than merely make impromptu remarks on the subject. As such, Teddy began to long once again for the national stage. As McKinley neared what seemed to be a surefire bid to gain reelection, Teddy was hopeful that he could leave his role as governor behind in favor of an appointment as part of McKinley's Cabinet, perhaps in a role similar to when he was the assistant secretary of the navy.

But the true opening for Teddy's return to the national stage would come with the untimely death of the man who had been McKinley's vice president, Garret Hobart. Hobart unexpectedly passed away in November of 1899 while McKinley was in the process of gearing up for reelection. It wasn't long before party leaders began to look toward Teddy Roosevelt as a possible pick for the ticket.

Knowing that the office of vice president was a largely idle one, Teddy, at first, hesitated and considered running for another term as governor of New York instead. Meanwhile, McKinley was somewhat ambivalent about the whole thing. So, instead of making a declaration one way or the other, he decided to leave the decision up to the delegates at the upcoming Republican National Convention in the summer of 1900. McKinley, after all, was known for being a very shrewd politician, and he wouldn't make such an important decision unless he knew there was a large groundswell of support for it. On the surface, McKinley did like the idea since he intuitively knew that the rough and tumble populism of Teddy did well to compliment his own more reserved nature. And other members of the party seemed to echo this sentiment. It was felt that Teddy's war record and his popularity with both East Coast New Yorkers and Western ranch hands would help the Republicans secure several states that might have otherwise gone to the Democrat camp.

With everyone in the party seemingly lining up to make Teddy the vice-presidential nominee, all that really remained was to get Teddy himself on board with the effort. Teddy had, at one point, considered rejecting the nomination outright, but in the end, even this tough old Rough Rider had to succumb to party pressure. Teddy knew that if he were to reject such a strong calling, he would most likely never be able to live it down.

Party boss Thomas Platt, who had been instrumental in Roosevelt's nomination, had famously quipped at the time, "Roosevelt might as well stand under Niagara Falls and try to spit water back as to stop his nomination." And he was right, for, in the end, the delegates at the convention gave Teddy the nomination by a landslide. Teddy acknowledged as much, stating, "I believe it all for the best...I should be a conceited fool if I was discontented with the nomination when it came in such a fashion."

Teddy accepted the nomination and then proceeded to invest himself in the 1900 presidential campaign with his trademark gusto. He barnstormed the country by train, stopping at all manner of locales, often dressed in Rough Rider regalia to the thrill of those who gathered to hear him speak. During his speeches, Teddy predictably hammered away at the need of securing America's overseas territorial gains, as well as hammering away at corrupt and unfair business practices such as the ones he dealt with while as governor of New York.

His efforts appeared to have paid off quite handsomely because, by the time the ballots were cast in November of 1900, William McKinley had won by a landslide. It was a landslide victory both in the electoral college and by sheer vote count, with the McKinley-Roosevelt ticket winning the popular vote by over 850,000 votes.

So, at just 42 years of age, Teddy was now the second-most powerful person in the United States. As high as this station was, it was an absolute dead end for most politicians. Most, including friends and enemies alike, fully expected Teddy to live out his term as vice president in relative obscurity. But fate would intervene on Teddy Roosevelt's behalf sooner rather than later.

Chapter 5 – A Square Deal for Every Man

Although Teddy took a rather pessimistic view of what his time as vice president might bring him, others were absolutely giddy with the possibilities. In fact, as soon as Roosevelt was sworn into office on March 4th, 1901, the nation had become rife with murmurings of a possible future run for president, with Roosevelt's name at the top of the ticket. But for Teddy himself, he viewed the vice presidency as not so much a springboard but a ball and chain that kept him bound.

Wishing to free himself from the constraints of a limited office, Teddy was absent from Washington much of the time, pursuing various other activities. During his first year as vice president, he busied himself by giving speeches at prestigious institutions, such as Yale and Harvard, as well as coming up with ideas and events for the Long Island Bible Society. Completely bored with the lack of work the office of the vice presidency provided, at one point, Teddy even contemplated the staging of a grizzly bear hunt in Colorado.

His days of boredom would come to a swift end, however, when on September 6th, 1901, an armed assailant by the name of Leon Czolgosz opened fire on William McKinley. President McKinley was presiding over an event in Buffalo, New York, when the incident occurred. Seeing Leon in the crowd, McKinley had extended a hand to shake the man's hand but was treated with a bullet instead.

The gunman was a political agitator known as an "anarchist" and was indeed hoping to create pandemonium by assassinating McKinley. President McKinley was hit two times, receiving what would ultimately be mortal wounds, as the bullets tore open his abdomen. Immediately after the gunman opened fire, fast-acting citizens tackled the shooter, and in their outrage, they were on the verge of dispensing their own version of justice right there on the spot. It was only the words of McKinley himself that stopped them, as he pleaded with the crowd not to harm the man they held in their custody. Just and equitable until the end, it was in this way that President McKinley ensured that his own killer would have a fair trial. Leon would ultimately be convicted for his crime and face execution by way of the electric chair. Teddy was at an engagement in Vermont when the shooting occurred, but he made sure to rush over as soon as he heard the news.

Teddy was just as surprised as anyone else at what had occurred, but at the time, he did not expect McKinley to perish. His wounds were serious, but most believed that he would recover from them. Teddy believed this to be true, as he made the decision to depart and head to a retreat in the Adirondack Mountains where his family was staying. This was supposedly out of a desire to send a clear signal to the public that McKinley was going to pull through.

But just a few days later, on September 12th, McKinley's health began to deteriorate rapidly. Teddy was immediately informed of the dire state of the president by a telegram sent from McKinley's personal secretary, George Cortelyou. Teddy, unsure of what to do, decided to wait for another update on McKinley's condition before making another trip back to Buffalo.

The latest report—this one more urgent than before—would reach Teddy near midnight while he and his family were sleeping. Teddy's slumber was interrupted with the news that McKinley was slipping fast and most likely didn't have much time left. Realizing that McKinley's hour had come, Roosevelt rushed back once again to Buffalo. McKinley would die on the morning of September 14th, 1901, while Teddy was still in transit, making 42-year-old Theodore Roosevelt, the new president of the United States.

Upon assuming the presidency, Teddy made sure that he would not rock the boat. Out of respect for the slain McKinley, he vowed, "It shall be my aim to continue absolutely unbroken the policy of President McKinley." This was at least some small assurance for those that were wary of what the rough and tumble Rough Rider might bring to the presidency.

Putting words to action, Roosevelt also ensured that he maintained the Cabinet that McKinley already had in place, rather than cleaning house upon his arrival. One of the first challenges he faced in the wake of McKinley's death was to reassure a jittery stock market, whose investors began to reconsider their investments. This was something Teddy considered to be imperative, not simply for the market but also for the sake of his own prestige as the new president. As he allegedly confided with reporter Herman Kohlsaat at the time, "I don't care a damn about stocks and bonds, but I don't want to see them go down the first day I am President!" Fortunately for Teddy, the stock market managed to calm itself down, but shortly thereafter, he was in for an uproar of an entirely different kind that genuinely took him by surprise.

Shortly before the death of McKinley, Theodore Roosevelt had become acquainted with the famous African American leader, innovator, and educator Booker T. Washington. Washington was the founder of the esteemed Tuskegee Institute and had invited then-Vice President Teddy Roosevelt to pay a visit to the school. Teddy accepted the invitation without hesitation. The assassination of President McKinley had delayed those plans, however, but Teddy extended an invitation for Booker to personally pay him a visit at the White House. Booker T. Washington, not one to miss an opportunity, readily accepted and promptly met up with Teddy on October 16th, 1901.

By all accounts, the meeting was a good one. Teddy and Booker held mutual respect and high regard for each other. Both men were self-starters, full of energy, ideas, and ambition. The two men seemed to be natural allies, and they should have been the best of friends. But sadly, the newspapers of the Deep South just didn't see it that way. And it wasn't long before they started hurling abuse Teddy's way.

Without even knowing what the meeting had been about, the *Memphis Scimitar*, for example, declared the encounter as "the most damnable outrage ever perpetrated by any citizen of the United States." Teddy was quite honestly shocked and dumbfounded by the pushback he received from this one simple meeting. At first, Teddy was defiant and sought to use the bully pulpit of the presidency to push back against those who would criticize him for meeting with Booker T. Washington. As Teddy declared at the time, "The idiot or vicious bourbon element of the South is crazy because I have had Booker T. Washington to dine. I shall have him to dine just as often as I please." But soon, the opposition from the South and even some from the North was too much of a load for Teddy to bear. And even though he personally expressed his sincere regret to Booker in private, he began to distance himself from Booker in public in order to avoid further political fallout.

As regrettable as the situation was, Teddy's steely navigation through the minefield he was in seemed to proffer some success in the following midterm elections, with the Republicans managing to maintain their hold of Congress. In the meantime, Roosevelt was doing his best to shore up support among Republican representatives, such as Senators Nelson Aldrich, Orville Platt, John Spooner, and William Allison, all of whom were real movers and shakers within the party at the time.

Although Teddy was more than willing to go against the establishment, he had long learned the value of getting in good with Washington insiders. As such, he was sure to consult with them when he enacted one of his biggest contributions to the country in the form of the creation of the Bureau of Corporations and the United States

Department of Commerce and Labor, both of which would be created in 1903.

At this time, heavy industry was the name of the game, but Theodore was concerned that only a few wealthy industrialists were profiting while the average worker suffered. He felt that the powerful owners of all the factories, warehouses, and corporations needed to be regulated so that they were made to provide better conditions for their employees. A major means of doing this was for Teddy to go after the so-called "trusts." These trusts were the stranglehold monopolies that big business had over certain industries. And in Teddy's day, one of the biggest of these corporate trusts was that of J.P. Morgan's Northern Securities Company. This was a massive railroad conglomerate that had grown enormously by the early 1900s, and it was throwing its weight around to take ownership of a large chunk of all the rail lines in the country.

Teddy sought to bust this trust, and he did so by taking his case to the Supreme Court in 1903. The court ultimately agreed with the president and deemed that the Northern Securities Company had overreached itself and had wrongfully sought to curtail free trade. During his time in office, Teddy would become known as a true "trust buster," breaking up more than forty similar monopolies and, by so doing, restoring equilibrium to American business.

In these efforts, Roosevelt had proven himself to be a champion of the public who was looking out for the "little guy." However, this image would be severely tested when the nation's economy was threatened by a massive coal miner's strike. For the modern reader, such a strike may not seem like much of a big deal. But back in 1902, coal was a vital resource, and when the coal miners were threatening to shut down production of coal, it was nothing less than a national emergency.

The strikers had been asking for a wage increase, as well as their general workday to be reduced to just eight hours and their union to be officially recognized. Their bosses, meanwhile, didn't want to supply anything of the sort. The ensuing standoff sent coal prices through the roof, and as a result, many Americans would become at risk of not being able to heat their homes for the winter.

Roosevelt, seeking to stave off disaster, ordered representatives of both parties to meet with him at the White House to resolve their differences. The owners of the mines proved rather obstinate, however, and would not come to an agreement. Instead of a peaceful solution, they asked for the army to be sent in to stop the strike.

However, Teddy would not take that as a solution, and he was quick to tell those in charge of the mines that if they didn't come to an agreement with their workers, he would indeed send in the troops. But he wouldn't send them to go after the striking workers; instead, they would forcibly take control of the mines at the expense of the owners. This was what finally got the bosses of the mines to sing a different tune.

Soon they were allowing Teddy to create a special commission to arbitrate the matter and even agreeing to put one of the union officials on the board. Roosevelt had flexed a little muscle and managed to get a desirable result. Teddy, happy with the outcome, went on the record to state, "My action on labor should always be considered in connection with my action as regards capital, and both are reducible to my favorite formula—a square deal for every man."

Chapter 6 – The Panama Canal and a Bid for Reelection

During the first few years of his first term as president, Teddy had achieved much. He had stood up to big business, and he had helped the American worker. Teddy had offered his square deal to anyone who was willing to accept it, and the nation was better for it. He had indeed accomplished quite a bit, but by the summer of 1903, he was in serious need of a break from Washington.

In those days, the summer months in DC could be particularly stifling without the advent of air conditioning. As such, Teddy was more than ready to get back to his family in the cooler confines of Oyster Bay, New York. Here, he would spend the next three months getting reacquainted with friends, family and, most especially, his love for the outdoors.

Roosevelt spent his summer days riding horses, relaxing in rowboats, and going on picnics with his wife. His children—with the exception of Alice—were also present and, as Teddy put it, "gloriously underfoot." But it was little Quentin, Teddy's youngest son, who would pester Teddy the most during his summer sojourn. Quentin was said to have followed in the footsteps of his father so closely that he became the best of friends with the Secret Service detail who watched over his dad.

But even during his summer vacation, Teddy still kept abreast of all manner of intrigue. This was due to the constant stream of visitors who would come to Sagamore Hill to consult with Teddy on a wide variety of issues. Even when it seemed like Teddy was taking a break, he was, in reality, just as engaged and plugged in as ever. One can only imagine how much more of a working vacation it probably would have been if only he had access to email and smartphones.

By the time Teddy returned to DC in the fall of 1903, he had plenty of matters to resolve. Chief among them was the fact that the so-called "tariff lobby" in DC had been challenging the Cuban reciprocity treaty that planned to decrease the tax on commerce coming out of Cuba while reducing duties on goods exported to the island. While his critics objected to the agreement from an economic perspective, Teddy insisted that they were important in order to maintain "hemispheric security." He felt that it would be much better for Cuba to be the active trading partner of the United States than to be led into agreements with other foreign powers. As such, Teddy felt that it was imperative that US markets remain open to Cuba.

Teddy, like always, was seeking security in America's international space. And he felt that keeping Cuba on good terms with the United States remained crucial to this goal. Another area of concern for Teddy was the close proximity of Cuba to the Central American isthmus, the land bridge that connected North America and South America. Teddy had long envisioned a canal being constructed across this landmass in order to better aid the deployment of the US Navy. In these efforts, Cuba would be a logical staging area.

Ever since his days as the assistant secretary of the navy, Roosevelt had found himself greatly concerned and preoccupied with the readiness of America's fleet. The great imperial powers of the day had empires that stretched into both the Atlantic and the Pacific. Teddy, therefore, felt that it was absolutely crucial to gain dominance on the waters surrounding America's domain. In order to achieve this supremacy, the US Navy needed to be able to pool its resources from one side of the mainland to the other at a moment's notice, and only a canal would allow them to do so. It was for this reason that Teddy began to work toward what would become known as the Panama Canal. It was the region of Panama that held the narrowest body of land in all of the Americas, spanning just some fifty miles wide, that tenuously connected North and South America.

The idea was to cut through this land bridge, create a canal, and allow it to fill with water so that the US Navy would have a means of quickly moving ships from one side of the Americas to the other. At that time, Panama was actually a part of the Republic of Colombia. Teddy's secretary of state, John Hay, was able to broker an agreement with the Colombians, which allowed the US to lease a narrow strip of land across Panama—just enough to dig out a functional canal.

The original deal promised to give the Colombians some ten million in gold as a down payment, along with a yearly rent for $250,000. This was not a bad deal for the early 1900s, but the Colombians proved to be some rather shrewd negotiators and decided to continue haggling with the Americans for even better terms. The negotiations were disrupted, however, when Colombia experienced an internal revolution, in which Panama split from Colombia.

Roosevelt, perhaps the shrewdest negotiator of all, was quick to recognize Panama as its own country and carry on negotiations with the new Panamanian government rather than the Colombians. The Panamanian Revolution began on November 3rd, 1903, and as soon as it had erupted, Teddy immediately dispatched a battleship to the area in order to circumvent any potential Colombian incursions. Although Teddy was not responsible for starting the revolution, he was indeed involved in ensuring its success. However, this impulsive backing would not soon be forgotten by the Colombians.

At any rate, it would take about a decade of hard labor to make the Panama Canal fully operational for the US Navy, but the end result was an engineering wonder that would prove crucial during the two world wars that lay ahead in America's future. With this great feat in motion, Teddy felt that he was well poised to begin his campaign for the 1904 presidential election.

The State of the Union Address that he gave in December of 1903, in fact, could have almost been mistaken for an outright campaign speech. Roosevelt opened the speech by touting his accomplishments, declaring, "This country is to be congratulated on the amount of substantial achievement which has marked the past year both as regards our foreign and as regards our domestic policy."

He then spent a good chunk of the rest of this speech laying out the case for why he had gone forward with the Panama Canal project. In it, he detailed a bit of the region's chaotic history. He cited the instance of several riots, rebellions, insurrections, and revolutions that had occurred since 1850 as an indication that the previous controller of the region, Colombia, was "utterly incapable of keeping order on the Isthmus." Teddy argued that Colombia had its chance to maintain order in Panama and had failed. According to him, it was now America's turn to partner with the new Panamanian government to make the best of the situation. This was a deal that, of course, included the much-vaunted Panama Canal that Teddy and his supporters had wanted all along. Teddy stressed that it was in America's interest to do so and that the nation would be greatly disadvantaged if it did not.

President Roosevelt hoped that all of the benefits that he outlined in his State of the Union Address would be enough to convince any doubters that he was indeed the right man for the job. This, of course, is part and parcel to any president's State of the Union Address, but all the more so for Teddy, considering how it was that he came to be president in the first place.

As any of the so-called "accidental presidents," those who came into the presidency only by virtue of the demise of the top man on their ticket, Teddy was a bit insecure about his hold on the position. He would not feel completely comfortable with the role of president until he managed to win his own presidential campaign. Although

Teddy had a wellspring of support from his base, convincing some of the party bosses was another matter. There had been decided displeasure present among some of the corporate elite over Teddy's efforts to aid the coal miners in the massive coal mine strikes of 1902. Some had even gone so far as to label Teddy a "dangerous radical." But despite these misgivings, even his detractors in the party realized that there was no way they could substitute another candidate for Theodore Roosevelt.

After easily securing the Republican nomination, one of the first things to establish was who Teddy's vice president would be. Since becoming president, Teddy served his term with no vice president of his own. Now that the moment had come to find a contender for the office, he wanted to choose someone whom he thought would be a good match for the ticket. He initially favored politician Robert R. Hill, but in the end, it was Indiana Senator Charles Warren Fairbanks who was chosen for the job.

At any rate, the fall of 1904 had Teddy once again barnstorming the country to tout what he declared to be both domestic and international success stories. The economy was good, and Roosevelt told the average citizen that if they elected him for another four years, it would be even better. His subsequent campaign speeches spoke in simple and direct terms that the average voter could easily understand.

In brief, Teddy promised prosperity at home and respect among the other great nations abroad. One thing that seemed to stymie some of his supporters, and even bring on the age-old hated political accusation of "flipflopping" on the issues, was the fact that Roosevelt at times criticized both corporations and labor unions in equal measure. This made both big business and the unions question whose side Teddy was really stumping for. This was a fact that his Democrat opponent Alton Parker was sure to take full advantage of. But Roosevelt saw things differently. He didn't believe that he was on either the corporations' or the unionists' side; he was merely trying to get both to act as fair and equal as possible. Whether it was a corporation or the average worker, Roosevelt believed in "a square deal for every man."

Although, by all accounts, Roosevelt appeared to be a solid contender, as election day neared, he became uncharacteristically nervous. As he tellingly stated at the time, "I shall be confident of the result only after the votes are counted."

But Roosevelt needn't worry, for by the time that the votes were counted on election day, it was clear that Teddy was in for a landslide win. He secured 336 electoral votes, compared to his Democrat opponent's mere 140. Teddy also handily won the popular vote with 7.6 million against Alton Parker's 5.1 million. A victorious Teddy had indeed secured another term in office, and he did so decisively.

Chapter 7 – Two Weddings and a Second Term

Teddy was inaugurated into his new term as president in March of 1905. As might be expected with someone as grandiose as Teddy Roosevelt, it was a grand affair. Interestingly enough, another pair of famous Roosevelts who would one day reside in the White House were in attendance that day as well. Teddy's niece, Anna Eleanor Roosevelt, along with her soon-to-be husband, Franklin Delano Roosevelt, were in the crowd of well-wishers.

While Eleanor was a close relative of Teddy, Franklin was only distantly related. He was, in fact, Eleanor's fifth cousin. Nevertheless, the two had met and fallen in love, and shortly after Teddy's inauguration, the young power couple would be officially wed. They married on March 17th, with Teddy not only attending but actually being the man to "give the bride away" for the occasion. Since Eleanor's father, Teddy's brother Elliott Roosevelt, had perished years before, Teddy was once again the man of the hour.

Teddy was indeed a man for all occasions, but none captivated him more than international politics. One of the first incidents that really commanded his attention were developments in what had been an ongoing conflict between Japan and Russia. Known as the Russo-

Japanese War, this conflagration in the East had erupted in 1904 and was coming to its conclusion in the spring of 1905. Roosevelt had been cautiously following the events from a distance. And although he wouldn't admit it to anyone in public, he had privately confided with a select few that he was hoping that Japan might win. In Teddy's mind, the Russian Empire had overreached itself and needed to be taught a lesson. But on the other hand, Teddy was sagacious enough to realize that with Japan as the most powerful neighbor of the US in the Pacific, a victory with Russia would signal further Japanese expansion toward America, and with that came the very real potential for conflict.

As the war heated up, Japan was the first to score a major victory by seizing Port Arthur from the Russians in February of 1905. They followed this success by sending a land invasion force into Manchuria shortly after. As stunning as their defeat was in these exchanges, the Russians were still holding out the hope that their Baltic Fleet would be able to stop the Japanese advance. The only trouble was the Baltic Fleet was trapped *in the Baltic!* In order to get their naval craft in place, the Russian ships had to take a cumbersome route that had them navigating all the way around the tip of Africa and through the Indian Ocean before they could intercept the Japanese in the Pacific. This delay gave Japan extra time to prepare while putting significant wear and tear on the Russian ships and their exhausted crew. By the time the fleet arrived in May of 1905, they had practically sailed right into the jaws of defeat. Still, Japan shocked the world by making short work of this fleet, literally blowing the ships out of the water as they engaged them head-on in the Tsushima Strait. This was the calamity that would eventually bring Russia to its knees. However, a rather cautious and merciful Japan, not wishing to take things any further, agreed to meet them at the negotiating table.

And, as fate would have it, it was none other than Teddy Roosevelt who was tapped to be the great intermediary between the two warring powers. Japan had, in fact, directly requested Roosevelt to serve in this capacity. Initially, Washington DC was proposed as the most likely meeting grounds for these talks. However, it was Teddy who suggested that DC in the summer months was just too humid and uncomfortable, so instead, he suggested that the two parties meet in New Hampshire.

As well as allowing for cooler, more comfortable weather, this change of venue was also useful in getting away from the glare of the press, which would have been absolutely swarming the White House had they decided to hold the talks in DC. As part of the peace process, Japan was asking for recognition of newly gleaned territories, such as Korea and Manchuria, as well as Port Arthur and a portion of Sakhalin Island. But along with being ceded these territorial gains, Japan was also demanding that Russia pay an indemnity, or a sum of money, in order to compensate Japan for the expenses it had accrued during the conflict. Teddy, who saw Russia as the real bully at the table, had sympathy for Japan, but he knew that the humiliation of having to pay money to the Japanese was just too much for the Russians to bear. Teddy knew that in order to broker a real and lasting peace, he would have to get the Japanese to drop this part of the bargain.

As both sides seemed to dig in, Teddy thought that the whole deal was about to fall through, but at the very last minute, Japan agreed to forego any demand of financial reimbursement from Russia. The Japanese government had shrewdly estimated that a prolonged conflict with Russia would drain their coffers much worse than not receiving an indemnity and, therefore, decided to quit while they were still ahead.

The peace agreement between the two warring empires was finally settled with the Treaty of Portsmouth, which was signed on September 5th, 1905. Teddy, for one, was absolutely overjoyed at the outcome. He was so pleased with the agreeableness of Japan, in particular, that he sent a personal message to the Japanese emperor in which he thanked him for his "wisdom and magnanimity."

Teddy was certainly pleased with the results, and so was much of the rest of the world, so much so that Roosevelt would ultimately receive a Nobel Peace Prize for his efforts. Demonstrating his ability to be a true Renaissance man, Teddy appeared to be just as good at making peace as he had been at making war. With this international squabble taken care of, Roosevelt began to once again turn his gaze inward to domestic policy.

In particular, he turned to an issue that he had championed in the past—more streamlined regulations for US railroads. These efforts would culminate in the 1906 Hepburn Act, which dictated that the Interstate Commerce Commission would have the last say when it came to how much shippers, as well as passengers, would be charged for the use of the rails. This was meant to be a check on big money corporations that would attempt to monopolize the market and price gouge access to it.

Along with these efforts in reform, Teddy also presided over the passage of legislation to better regulate food and medication. It's Teddy Roosevelt that Americans can thank for the relative assurance that the food they eat and the medications they take are safe for consumption, for it was President Roosevelt who set in motion the "Pure Food and Drug Act." It was this act, which was passed in 1906, that paved the way for the establishment of the Food and Drug Administration (FDA). This was not an easy thing to do, considering the fact that several druggists and food manufacturers lobbied Congress to reject the legislation, claiming that their "liberty and their property" were at stake. Teddy persevered, however, until the Pure Food and Drug Act was made into law.

Right on the heels of this initiative, Teddy enacted the Federal Meat Inspection Act. The meat industry was something that Teddy knew a little about from his days as a rancher. But while he could relate to those who earned their living from the business, he also wanted to be sure that the country's food supply was safe. And it was in light of explosive reports of malpractice from the major meat packing industries that galvanized Teddy into action.

Among the grievances, it had apparently been discovered that some meat processing facilities refused to throw out old meat. Incredibly enough, it was said that spoiled meat had simply been dyed with food coloring in order to make it look fresh. Even more shocking than this were the criticisms of worker safety, which alleged that chopped hands, fingers, and the like from workplace accidents occasionally became processed with the meat. Let alone the hazard to the workers, the incidents suggested that at least a small percentage of packaged meat might actually have human flesh mixed in with them. Teddy was just as disgusted by these findings as the rest of the country, and he was determined to do something about it. He was the president who finally put down adequate enough legislation to make sure that the people responsible for producing the nation's meat valued safety and quality as much as they did their profits.

It was the meat inspection rules that Teddy Roosevelt put in place that finally got meat packing plants to properly maintain their produce. So, yes, when you bite into a hamburger at any given American fast-food joint or open up a can of SPAM at home, you can most certainly thank Teddy Roosevelt for the ensured quality of the meat you are consuming.

During this period, Teddy, the great frontiersman, was also instrumental in conserving what remained of America's forests. It was President Theodore Roosevelt, after all, who created some 150 million acres worth of national parks, forests, and nature preserves. While he was at it, he also created the department of the United States Forest Service, which was established in 1905, and declared eighteen separate sites as national monuments. In many ways, Teddy, the rugged Rough Rider who loved the great outdoors, was an environmentalist before most had even conceived of the concept.

Despite all these happenings on the national stage, Teddy also had plenty to do on the home front concerning his own personal family. His daughter Alice was 22 years old at the time, and she had been seeing a congressman, some fifteen years her senior, by the name of Nicholas Longworth.

Although Teddy had some reservations about the age gap, he slowly warmed to Nicholas, and perhaps thinking that marriage would help stabilize his somewhat troubled daughter, he eventually gave his blessing to the union. Their wedding was held in February of 1906. Teddy was once again giving away a bride, just as he had done with Eleanor Roosevelt two years before, except this time, it was his eldest daughter that he was seeing off.

Despite the rocky relationship Alice had with her parents, it was a caring and tender moment that they shared together. Teddy, seemingly overwhelmed with sentimental attachment to Alice, seemed almost on the verge of tears when he gave his daughter away. But perhaps the biggest and most welcome moment was when, after the vows were exchanged, Alice came right up to her stepmother Edith and gave her a big hug.

Although Edith had been a part of Alice's life since she was a baby, their relationship was, at times, a frosty one. This show of warmth and affection was indeed refreshing for them both. What wasn't so refreshing for Teddy was finding out a few weeks after the wedding that his eldest son and namesake, Ted, was on the verge of failing all of his classes at Harvard.

Ted Jr. had just started up at his father's alma mater Harvard when Teddy was notified by the dean that his son had been put on academic probation. President Roosevelt was mortified. He had placed high hopes in all of his children, but he had especially hoped that his eldest son would be successful in life. Alarmed at these developments, he quickly fired off a stern missive to Ted that ordered him to refocus his efforts on his studies. Teddy's correspondence came with the blunt warning, "It is of no use being popular in the class if you are going to be dropped out of the class."

Despite his son's dalliances at Harvard, 1906 began as a relatively good year for Teddy. As summer approached, however, storm clouds began to appear over a former pet project of the old Rough Rider—the newly independent former Spanish colony of Cuba. Having said that, one has to be careful when referring to early 20th-century Cuba as an independent nation. While the Americans did indeed help ensure its independence from Spain, it was, in many ways, still highly dependent upon its powerful neighbor, the United States. And when Cuba began to look as if it were on the brink of civil war in 1906, the fledgling Cuban government looked toward the US to quell the violence.

The trouble began shortly after the first president of the newly christened Republic of Cuba, Tomás Estrada Palma, was reelected. Palma was said to have defeated his opponent, José Miguel Gómez, but the election was widely held as being corrupt, and accusations of ballot stuffing and other voting irregularities boiled over into what became known as the "anti-Palma" insurgency.

As things grew increasingly precarious for Palma's government, he began to look toward the US for support, and by the fall of 1906, Palma and his associates were requesting all-out American intervention. This was not something that Teddy, nor hardly anyone else in the American government, desired. Teddy himself knew full well that if America had to force its hand and send troops into Cuba, it wouldn't be long before they would be viewed as unwanted colonial occupiers.

Before sending in the troops, Teddy thought it more prudent to send in his secretary of war, William Taft. Taft had been a holdover from the McKinley administration, and he had Teddy's full confidence in his judgment. Teddy went as far as to tell Taft that he would be given permission to call upon American military might if needed, but at the same time, he made sure to stress that under no circumstances should any measure be referenced as an "intervention." In case a little manpower might be needed, Teddy instructed Taft, "Simply say that they are landed to save life and property in Havana." Vested with this power, Taft attempted to negotiate a solution between the two camps, but Palma began to drag his feet, insisting that the US militarily intervene to get rid of his opposition. This provoked strong words from President Roosevelt, who told Palma in no uncertain terms, "It is evident that under existing circumstances your government cannot stand and that to attempt to maintain it or to dictate your own terms about the new government merely means disaster and perhaps ruin for Cuba."

Roosevelt then went on to say, "I adjure you for the sake of your own fair fame not so to conduct yourself that the responsibility, if such there be for the death of the republic, can be put at your door." It was in light of Palma's perceived obstinance to negotiation that Teddy began to look more favorably to the anti-Palma insurgency. But Taft opined with an intervention of his own and painted the insurgents in the starkest of terms to the president. Taft claimed that even the "mere thought of handing the government over to them made him shiver at the consequences."

Rather than falling in line with US demands, President Palma, when he realized that the US was not going to side with him, simply resigned instead, leaving office on September 28th, 1906. In the power vacuum that ensued, Taft took the initiative that Teddy had given him and installed himself as the "provisional governor of Cuba." The US Navy, meanwhile, landed troops on the shores of Cuba—much like Roosevelt had envisioned—in the name of protecting life and property.

At this point, the anti-Palma insurgents were so happy to have gotten rid of President Palma that they welcomed the American presence with open arms. From this point on, the Americans began to construct bases and focus on improving infrastructure, including that of the infamous Guantanamo Bay. Taft would then hand the baton over to an American diplomat by the name of Charles Edward Magoon.

Magoon took over as provisional governor on October 13th, 1906, and would stay on the job until a new election could be convened for the next Cuban president. That Cuban president ended up being none other than the former opposition leader, José Miguel Gómez, who was duly elected in 1908 and took office in January of 1909. With the new Cuban government established, the American troops left the following month.

By the end of Teddy's own term in 1908, he had accomplished much, and many expected him to accomplish even more. But Roosevelt had seemingly sealed his own fate back in 1904 when he declared that he would not run again for the office of president. He would soon come to regret those remarks.

Chapter 8 – The Lead-Up to a Political Apocalypse

Teddy came into office after the death of President William McKinley in September of 1901, serving out the remaining three and a half years that the assassinated president had been cheated out of. If this could be considered Teddy's first term, his victory in the 1904 presidential election was his second term. Therefore, if Teddy ran again in 1908, it would have been in pursuit of his third term.

Teddy, a stickler for tradition, wished to observe the long-standing habit of presidents to only serve two terms. It is important to note that although this was a long-standing tradition, in Teddy's day, it was not yet a mandatory law to have term limits on the presidency. It was, in fact, Teddy's own distant relative, Franklin Delano Roosevelt, who would go very much beyond the two-term tradition by being elected an unprecedented four times throughout the 1930s and 1940s.

Despite the fact that Teddy was determined not to embark upon a third run, he was more than ready to anoint his would-be successor. And the man he had in mind for the job was William Howard Taft. Taft had worked as a judge in the state of Ohio before becoming the governor of the American territory of the Philippines. The placement of Taft as governor of the Philippines came at the behest of President

McKinley in 1900, shortly after the islands had become a US territory. Taft had actually been hoping that McKinley would place him as a judge on the Supreme Court, but he was given the governorship instead. Taft had also served as the secretary of war during Teddy's second term, where events in Cuba had Taft serving as a provisional governor once again, this time in a brief stint for the Cubans. It was during his time as secretary of war that Teddy had developed a strong bond with Taft.

Perhaps, most importantly, Taft was a strident supporter of most of Teddy's policies, which was a fact that would in the ensuing years become both a blessing and a curse, with some writing Taft off as nothing more than a yes-man-styled lackey of Teddy's. They even invented a humorous acronym out of his name in order to mock him. These detractors suggested that TAFT actually stood for "Take Advice from Teddy."

Not everyone in the party was happy with the idea of this groomed heir apparent, and in the lead-up to Taft's nomination as Teddy's successor, they made their displeasure known. Nevertheless, Taft went on to clinch the nomination as the Republican Party candidate. Taft was riding high on the popularity that the Roosevelt administration had gained, and as a consequence, Teddy's most important advice to Taft was simply to not rock the boat and keep his mouth shut. Or, as Teddy told him, "I believe you will be elected if we can keep things as they are; so be very careful to say nothing, not one sentence, that can be misconstrued, and that can give a handle for effective attacks." Taft, for the most part, kept to this "stay the course" strategy, and it paid off in November, with Taft winning the election by a large margin. Teddy was typically exuberant at the results, declaring, "The result is a great victory and a mighty good thing for the whole country. Naturally I am greatly pleased."

After handing over the reins of power to Taft, Teddy decided to allow the new president to "be his own man." And so that he wouldn't constantly be looking over his shoulder, Teddy resolved to go on an extended vacation. He actually ended up taking a safari tour of Africa, which was officially known as the Smithsonian-Roosevelt African Expedition.

Teddy declared this big game hunting excursion of his as a scientific endeavor. He had contacted the Smithsonian Museum before leaving and had promised to bring back stuffed specimens of the animals he shot so that they could be used at an exhibit in the museum. Teddy planned on only shooting one of each species, or at the most one male and one female. And so it was that Teddy envisioned himself taking down lions, elephants, and rhinoceros, all in the name of science. But those that knew him best fully realized the convenient cover story he had created, for they knew that Teddy valued the distance that this major trek would put between him and DC most of all. As stated above, Teddy hoped that this would give the new president some breathing room to stand on his own. However, Teddy also knew that if he stayed behind, journalists would constantly hound him about every action Taft might take, seeking to get his opinions and reactions. But in the African bush, Teddy would be safe from the political pundits.

Accompanying him in his descent into the wilderness was his son Kermit—just shy of twenty at the time—as well as a group of specialists documenting the findings along the way. Teddy, too, served to document the trip by keeping journal entries that he submitted to *Scribner's Magazine*, which were eventually published as a stand-alone piece called *African Game Trails: An Account of the African Wanderings of an American Hunter Naturalist.*

If Teddy's record can be trusted, it is said that by the summer of 1909, Teddy had quite a bit of wild game under his belt. Among other things, he had bagged two giraffes, six lions, a zebra, a hippo, and a rhinoceros, the latter of which he claimed had "charged viciously, and might have done mischief" had it not been stopped. After it was all said and done, Teddy was able to bring back 11,000 "specimens" for the museum.

Along with hunting, Teddy also became quite involved with the British colonial authorities. That part of Africa, then known as British

East Africa or the East Africa Protectorate—today as Kenya—was one of the jewels of the British Empire. Teddy was received well by the British in Nairobi, and his efforts were, if anything else, a great diplomatic coup for the Brits, for those he met in British East Africa would go back to Britain singing his praises.

The expedition came to a close in the spring of 1910, and much to the relief of Edith Roosevelt, she was reunited with Teddy and Kermit when they met up with her in Khartoum, Sudan, that March. From here, they traveled together to Egypt and then on over the Mediterranean to the European continent. This, in itself, became a kind of political safari, in which the Roosevelts were greeted as unofficial heads of state by delegations in the countries of Belgium, Holland, Germany, Italy, Austria Hungary, and Great Britain.

As can be deduced from a description he gave of his time at London's Buckingham Palace, it is clear that Teddy reveled in the attention he received. Teddy recalled the event, saying, "I have never attended a more hilarious banquet in my life. I have never seen so many knights. When I met a little bewizened [sic] person known as the King of Greece, he fairly wept out his troubles to me."

Even while Teddy was galivanting about overseas, he was being kept informed on Taft's progress by his own group of loyal Washington insiders. Chief among them was his old confidant, Senator Henry Cabot Lodge. It was from his pipeline of correspondence that Teddy had learned that Taft's presidency had not lived up to what he and others in the party had hoped.

Firstly, Taft had decided to clean house and get rid of some of Teddy's appointed staff. These appointments proved to be more pro-corporation than they were pro-worker or pro-American consumer, and as such, they clashed with the image that Teddy had tried to cultivate while he was in office. It wasn't long before several holdovers from Teddy's administration began to long for the days of Theodore Roosevelt. Or, as Lodge informed Teddy at the time, "There is a constantly growing thought of you and your return to the Presidency."

At first, Teddy was hesitant to get involved, as he remarked to another close associate after receiving these tidings, "It is a very ungracious thing for an ex-President to criticize his successor." Teddy would remain quiet about these developments for the rest of his tour overseas, but by the time he came back in the summer of 1910, many were still wondering if Teddy could somehow save them from their electoral woes in the upcoming midterm elections.

Teddy sailed into Staten Island on June 16th, 1910, to a hero's welcome. Upon his arrival, six battleships presented themselves in the harbor, and Teddy was greeted with an all-out 21-gun salute. As soon as Teddy was sighted on deck, those who crowded around the docks began cheering and shouting their unbridled praise and enthusiasm. After Teddy managed to make his way off the boat, he was driven down Broadway in what amounted to an extended parade replete with former Rough Riders, ranch hands, and other long time Theodore Roosevelt supporters.

Teddy had successfully made his triumphant return. But at the end of this triumphal march, one had to wonder—what did this mean for America? And perhaps none wondered more than President Howard Taft. Shortly after Teddy's arrival, Taft requested Teddy to meet with him at the White House. Taft was surprised to have his summons flatly turned down. Although not yet giving any sign of real displeasure with Taft, Teddy had firmly informed him, "I don't think it well for an ex-President to go to the White House, or indeed to go to Washington, except when he cannot help it."

But although he thought it imprudent to go to DC, Teddy soon came around to the idea of meeting up with Taft at his home in Beverly, Massachusetts. As Taft laid eyes on Teddy, he treated him like an old friend, grabbing his hands and declaring, "Ah, Theodore, it is good to see you." But after Roosevelt responded with an official, "How are you, Mr. President?" Taft seemed to feel the distance between them, and seeking to ameliorate it, he grabbed Teddy by the shoulder, and told him, "See here now, drop the 'Mr. President.'"

Teddy was adamant, however, and insisted, "Not at all. You must be Mr. President and I am Theodore. It must be that way."

A further indication of the frostiness that had developed between the two men occurred when Teddy asked the butler to bring him a "scotch and soda." For a man who rarely drank, it was rather obvious that Teddy was feeling uneasy and needed to calm his nerves. Nevertheless, as they persevered through their sometimes awkward conversation, the two men seemed to eventually come around.

It was once the conversation turned to Teddy's exploits that the old boisterous and entertaining Teddy Roosevelt came out, and he lost himself in the joy of relaying all of his riveting tails of pursuing lions in the African bush and chasing royals in the European courts. It would be just a brief reprieve, though, for after the current and former president parted ways, the cracks once again began to show. Political operatives spoke with Teddy practically on a daily basis to inform him of the latest political grievances that were being aired in the midst of what had become an interparty war.

The upcoming midterms would serve to bring these grumblings right out in the open, with devastating losses for the Republicans in both the House of Representatives and the Senate. In this disaster, the Republicans lost what had been a solid hold on the House of Representatives, losing some 58 congressional seats to the Democrats. And although the Republicans managed to maintain control over the Senate, it wasn't by much, with their previous 29-seat lead shrinking to just 10. Interestingly enough, one of those seats taken by the Democrats was none other than Franklin Delano Roosevelt.

At any rate, political rumblings in DC were one thing, but the midterms seemed, in many minds, to demonstrate the ill stewardship of the current commander-in-chief. This was the true turning point in which Teddy began to turn against Taft.

Shortly after the midterm election, a group of progressive Republicans, feeling thwarted by what they saw as Taft's failures, came together to form what they called the National Progressive Republican

League. It wasn't long before this oppositional group within the party began to look toward Teddy to champion their cause.

However, as disenchanted as Teddy was, he was not quite willing to completely break with the president of his own party. In the end, Roosevelt declined to be openly involved with the group, although he privately gave his blessing to their efforts. But he would soon do much more than that. Since his return to the United States, Teddy had struck up a new gig as a regular contributor to a publication called *The Outlook*. Here, he was able to voice his views on a great many things, and it wasn't long before progressivism came front and center. In the Spring of 1911, Teddy wrote several pieces in which he voiced his approval for what he termed to be the "great movement of our day, the Progressive Nationalist movement against privilege and in favor of an honest and effective political and industrial democracy."

Even with these musings, Teddy never dreamed of attempting to take the nomination from Taft in the upcoming 1912 presidential election. This didn't stop others from suggesting it, however, and in November 1911, calls were made by some of his fellow Republicans for Teddy to be nominated. As speculation began to grow as to whether or not Teddy would accept the nomination, critics began to crop up to remind everyone of Theodore's previous vow not to seek a third term.

While not coming out and saying he would actually run or not, Teddy responded to the critics with a very simple analogy, stating, "Frequently when asked to take another cup of coffee at breakfast, I say 'No thank you, I won't take another cup.' This does not mean that I intend never to take another cup of coffee during my life." In other words, Teddy was intimating that just because he said he wasn't going to seek a third term during one election cycle didn't mean he wouldn't seek it out in another. Teddy was basically insinuating that his pledge to not seek another term was in reference to a "third consecutive term." But now that he was out of office and had let someone else man the helm for a while, he suggested that he could indeed come back for a non-consecutive third term.

Teddy's private criticisms of Taft, although still somewhat coded, were decidedly harsher in nature. This was evidenced that December when Teddy remarked to a colleague, "I am really sorry for Taft, I am sure he means well, but he means well feebly, and he does not know how! He is utterly unfit for leadership, and this is a time when we need leadership."

So, while striking a sympathetic note to his former friend and successor, Teddy made clear his feelings that Taft was completely inept for the task at hand. By January of 1912, Teddy was cautiously hinting that he would be open to receiving the nomination himself by publicly stating, "If the people make a draft on me. I shall not decline to serve."

It was shortly after this declaration was made that Teddy appeared in front of a constitutional convention in Ohio, where he extolled progressive values and labeled himself as a progressive Republican. In the speech, he also went so far as to suggest that there should be a "popular review of state judicial decisions." This was a move that finally pushed the long-suffering Taft to the breaking point, with Taft declaring, "Such extremists are not progressives—they are political emotionalists or neurotics."

The idea that Teddy and his ilk were unhinged extremists was one that Taft and his allies would come to repeat, with some going so far as to suggest that Teddy himself was nothing more than a power-hungry megalomaniac. In light of these charges, a friend of Teddy's, Robert Grant, felt it necessary to go on the record to state, "I saw no signs of unusual excitement. He halts in his sentences occasionally; but from a layman's point of view there was nothing to suggest mental impairment, unless the combination of egotism, faith in his own doctrines, fondness for power and present hostility to Taft, can be termed symptomatic."

Still, Taft persisted that those who wished to convene panels to review the decisions of judges were at risk of "turning the United States into a replica of revolutionary France." Taft likened such things to the panels and committees of the French Revolution, which became so inflamed with their own opinions that they created a reign of terror. Teddy was characterized as a mad, rough-riding Robespierre, who was ready to march the rest of the Republicans off to the guillotine.

Teddy, of course, saw it differently, and he was quick to allege that the only reason someone would fear judicial review would be if they feared that the ill intentions of their justice department might come to light. Rather than the tyranny of an inflamed mob that Taft likened it to, Teddy insisted that it was simply an enactment of the will of the popular government. Teddy further declared that "Mr. Taft's position is perfectly clear. It is that we have in this country a special class of persons wiser than the people, who are above the people, who cannot be reached by the people, but who govern them and ought to govern them; and who protect various classes of the people from the whole people."

Teddy called his new platform "New Nationalism" and was soon taking his populist message right to the people. And it seemed to pay off. In all of the states that the Republican convention had delegates selected by primary voters, Roosevelt won big. He even managed to win Taft's own home state of Ohio. It was in the battleground state of Ohio, in fact, that some of the most bitter and rancorous exchanges between Taft and Teddy occurred.

Taft denounced Teddy as a "dangerous demagogue" and a "flatterer of the people." Teddy's rebuttal was vicious, with him calling Taft a "fathead" with an "intellect" that "fell slightly shy of a guinea pig." To Taft's humiliation, Teddy did go on to win Ohio. But even with this surge, the real choice would be made at the national convention by the party bosses, and most of these bosses were still firmly in Taft's corner.

In the end, Taft came into the convention with 411 delegates and Teddy with 367; this left 254 delegates still for the taking. The Republican National Convention made short work of this, however, handing off 235 to Taft and only 19 to Teddy, thereby guaranteeing Taft's nomination. When it became clear that Teddy was going to be "shut out" of the nomination, Teddy raced down to where the convention was being held in Chicago and stated to those gathered there that what he saw as the "perpetration of a great crime" should not stand.

Reminiscent of the polarizing language of today in which one candidate insinuates that the other will bring nothing but doom and gloom, Teddy seemed to suggest that the second term of Taft would quite literally bring about doomsday itself. He concluded his remarks in Chicago by stating, "We stand at Armageddon, and we battle for the Lord!" These were the stark terms that Teddy laid bare to his supporters, and he maintained that he was being cheated out of the nomination by Taft's crooked cronies. For Teddy, a political apocalypse was indeed at hand.

Chapter 9 – Teddy's Final Run and His River of Doubt

After being denied the Republican nomination, Teddy Roosevelt made his intentions very clear. He would make a bid for a third party run. Creating his own Progressive Party, Teddy stated, "I shall accept the progressive nomination on a progressive platform, and shall fight to the end, win or lose." Teddy's party would unofficially become known as the Bull Moose Party. It came to be known this due to an interview in which Teddy was questioned about his health. "I'm as fit as a bull moose," he retorted.

After his nomination with the Progressive Party, Teddy was now slated to run head-to-head with not only Taft but also the Democrat nominee, Woodrow Wilson. Wilson was the governor of New Jersey, who said that he, too, sought many of the reforms Teddy spoke of, but he didn't think that "direct controls" implemented by the federal government were necessary to achieve them.

Wilson was an intelligent and persuasive speaker, and Teddy—as much as he may have criticized him—knew that he faced a tough opponent. He knew this campaign would be especially hard due to the fact that he had basically just torn the Republican Party asunder between the progressive wing, which supported his third party movement, and the more conservative faction, which supported Taft.

Teddy, attempting to take them both out, tried to lump them together, claiming that they were both a part of the same corporate machine and often referring to them as if they were even on the same ticket, calling them "Taft-Wilson." This was obviously not the case, but it ended up being Taft that encountered the most serious challenge, as he lost supporters to Teddy and faced a domineering Democrat candidate in Wilson.

Teddy, meanwhile, took full advantage of this discord and kicked off his national campaign in the summer of 1912. He started off campaigning in New England that August before traveling all across the northern states and ending up all the way in California in September. On his trip back, he then went through some midwestern regions he missed and cut through parts of the southern states before heading home again in October.

Shortly thereafter, he returned to the Midwest and ended up in Milwaukee, Wisconsin, on October 14th. It was in Milwaukee, as Teddy was making his way to give a speech, that a man by the name of John Flammang Schrank stepped up to Teddy, pulled out a gun, and shot him. Fortunately for Teddy, the fact that he had his eyeglass case and a bundle of papers—his prepared speech—stuffed in front of his chest saved his life.

The bullet sliced through the eyeglass case and documents, and it was slowed down just enough to stop against Teddy's ribcage. One of his ribs was shattered in the process, but neither his lung nor any other vital organ was punctured. Teddy was knocked to the ground by the force of the gunshot all the same, but after regaining his wind, he stood up and actually came to the defense of his would-be assassin.

In a vein similar to McKinley, Teddy advised the crowd of people that had tackled the gunman, "Stand back! Don't hurt the man!" Roosevelt was then attended to by doctors who had rushed to the scene. They advised him that he should be taken to the hospital immediately. Teddy refused, however, declaring, "I will make this speech or die. It is one thing or the other." Teddy would later claim that he knew that the wound was not fatal since he wasn't "coughing up blood."

At any rate, the obstinance of Teddy won out, and he took the stage in the Milwaukee Auditorium as planned. With a bloody handkerchief pressed to his chest, Teddy announced to those assembled, "Friends, I shall ask you to be as quiet as possible. I don't know whether you fully understand that I have just been shot; but it takes more than that to kill a Bull Moose. The bullet is in me now, so that I cannot make a very long speech, but I will try my best."

Teddy then opened up the vest he was wearing in order to show his blood-drenched shirt underneath. The audience, of course, was shocked, but Teddy, not wanting to let them down for a moment, continued, "I have altogether too important things to think of to feel any concern over my own death; and now I cannot speak to you insincerely within five minutes of being shot. I am telling you the literal truth when I say that my concern is for many other things. It is not in the least for my own life. I want you to understand that I am ahead of the game, anyway."

Teddy then went on to state what almost sounded like his own eulogy, saying, "No man has had a happier life than I have led; a happier life in every way." He then advised the crowd, "Don't waste any sympathy on me. I have had an A-1 time in life and I am having it now." The audience, unsure if he was about to drop dead right before their eyes, held their breath in wonder as Teddy continued to speak for about an hour's time before he finally allowed himself to be rushed to the hospital.

During the course of his speech, he reminded the audience of what was at stake. He alleged that Taft had stolen the nomination from the people while asserting that Democrat Wilson was not a "true progressive." As his supporters cheered him on, he was certainly preaching to the choir that night. But many in the crowd, no matter how much they agreed with his sentiments, breathed a sigh of relief all the same when Teddy finally got off that stage and allowed himself to be taken to the emergency room.

Upon being taken in for treatment, the wound did indeed prove to be non-life threatening, and with proper care, Teddy was on the mend quickly. His wife Edith, as well as Alice, Ted, and Ethel, all came to visit him in the hospital. Of these, it was Edith that made the most memorable impression on reporters, with the way that she took charge of Teddy's care. As one reporter described it, "That sedate and determined woman, from the moment of her arrival in Chicago, took charge of affairs and reduced the Colonel to pitiable subjection. Up to her advent he was throwing bombshells into his doctors. The moment she arrived a hush fell upon T.R. He became as meek as Moses." Edith, no doubt recalling how McKinley, who at first was believed to be in recovery, had suddenly taken a turn for the worse, was desperate to ensure that the same fate did not occur to her husband.

Despite his injury, Teddy was actually enjoying himself fairly well in the hospital. He most certainly didn't appreciate the interruption from the campaign trail, but he was determined to make the best of it regardless. As he remarked to his sister Bamie, "Really the time in the hospital with Edith and the children here, has been a positive spree, and I have enjoyed it. Of course, I would like to have been in the campaign, but it can't be helped and there is no use crying over what can't be helped!"

Upon being discharged from the hospital, Teddy then went on to make a few more speeches before the voters cast their ballots that November. It was during one of these last rallying cries that Teddy laid out the stakes of the election as he saw them. He reasoned that neither the Republicans nor the Democrats were fit to be elected to the highest office in the land that election year. He proclaimed that it was only the Progressive Party that truly held American interests at heart. Teddy trumpeted, "We, and we alone, stand for the real right of the people to rule their own government."

The American public was truly mesmerized by Teddy Roosevelt. And after he withstood an assassin's bullet, the fascination only increased. But even after his stunning recovery, it still wasn't enough to enable Teddy to secure a win against both Taft and Wilson. In the end, the Democrat candidate received the most support from the divided electorate, and so, Woodrow Wilson would go on to become the next president of the United States.

Truth be told, if Teddy had received the nomination for the Republican Party, he likely would have won. It was largely the fact that Teddy and Taft split the vote between each other that allowed Wilson to hold the majority. Teddy received 4.1 million votes, and Taft had just 3.5 million. Compare that with Wilson's 6.3 million. If Teddy and Taft's votes were tallied together, it comes to well over seven million votes. So, if Teddy had received all of those Republican votes that went to Taft, it would have been a clear and decisive win.

Although Teddy had very much considered this outcome beforehand, he was still disheartened when it came to fruition, all the same. Nevertheless, he still put on a brave face for the Progressive Party. This was evidenced in January 1913 when he wrote a rousing missive to key members of the party, imploring them, "It is imperatively necessary for every true Progressive to make it clearly understood that this party has come to stay, and that under no circumstances will there be any amalgamation with either of the old parties."

Teddy urged his followers to hold true to progressive values on their own merits and to resist the urge to break rank and join the other two dominant parties. As much as Teddy put on a brave face for the Progressive Party, deep down, he knew that it was most likely a lost cause. He realized that unless they could chip at the Democrats and take some of their faithful party members and bring them to the Progressive fold, it was largely hopeless.

As he explained to his sister-in-law, Emily, at the time, "If the Democrats do well, then the reason for a Progressive Party will be so small that the ground may be swept from under our feet." However, besides venting to relatives when it came to his views on the future of the Progressive Party, Teddy kept his cards fairly close to his chest.

When he wasn't talking about politics, the spring of 1913 found him prodigiously writing about it and other matters, as he published his own autobiography in a serialized format. These were issued in several print newspapers over the next few months and finally found their way as a standalone book before the year was out.

Later that summer, Teddy decided to dust off his feet by taking his sons Quentin and Archibald for a tour of the Southwest. Here, Teddy was back in his old rough-riding element. In between the hunting and riding forays, Teddy actually reconnected with some of the men he had served with in days long gone by. After they had their fill of the West, Teddy then took his sons with him to Chicago, where he met up with Progressive Party leaders there.

Teddy and company then headed home, but they were barely in the door before Teddy started to contemplate his next move. Feeling like he needed a break from all the political intrigue that he had been knee-deep in, Teddy decided he wanted to leave the country. At first, he was considering another safari in Africa. His trip in 1910 had done much to relieve his anxieties, and he felt that a repeat just might be in order. But a visit from a certain Catholic priest, by the name of Father John Augustine Zahm, had Teddy looking in another part of the globe altogether.

Father Zahm had spent many years in the missionary field in South America. Teddy always wanted to go on an extended excursion in South America, and the tales that this priest told him absolutely astounded him. Teddy found himself enamored with the wild untamed wilderness that Zahm described. The South American continent held some of the most remote, untouched places on the planet. For someone who wanted to take a break from civilization, it must have seemed like just what the doctor had prescribed.

Excited by his conversation with Father Zahm, Teddy wasted no time in jumping on both the telephone and the telegraph to tie up all the loose ends that would be needed for his trip. After making contact with those that would be instrumental in making the expedition happen, it was determined that Teddy would take a ship to the Brazilian capital of Rio de Janeiro before traveling across land through Brazil, then on to Uruguay, Argentina, and finally Chile.

As part of the trip's itinerary, Roosevelt, who had just recently been made the president of the American Historical Association, was tasked with collecting specimens and artifacts from the trip. It was in this vein that Teddy decided that he would once again throw himself into the wild in search of specimens to be placed in museums. But the greatest find wouldn't be an artifact or an animal specimen; instead, it would be the rushing waters of a large waterway known as the "River of Doubt," which, at the time, was still uncharted territory.

As Teddy made all of these plans, his son Kermit, who was unemployed at the moment, eagerly enlisted to join his father. Out of all those who would volunteer for the trip, Kermit would become the most indispensable. It would later be recalled that when Teddy was at his lowest, darkest moment during the expedition, it was his only his son's encouragement that kept him going.

The undertaking of their journey was immense. Along the way, they battled the elements and all manner of wildlife. It was truly a lively, and downright deadly, assortment, which included plagues of parasitic pests, such as mosquitoes and ticks, as well as man-eating piranha and vampire bats swooping down over their heads. Navigating through this gauntlet would be difficult for anyone, let alone a man in his fifties still recovering from an assassination attempt. But Teddy and his crew persevered regardless.

Teddy's biggest problem occurred when he attempted to rescue a couple of canoes that had sailed out of their reach. The canoes were sent crashing against some rocks, and Teddy, believing them to be vital for the trip, didn't hesitate to chase after them. He jumped right into the water and managed to bring them to shore, but as he did so, he injured his leg. The injury he sustained became badly infected shortly after, and it led to Teddy contracting a dangerous fever.

According to his son Kermit's later recollection, Teddy had become delirious and began to speak incoherently.

At one point, however, his muddled thoughts cleared up enough for him to consider the dangerous nature of the group's dwindling supplies. It seems that Teddy came to a stark realization and pondered if it wouldn't be better if he was simply left for dead so that the others could get rid of the burden of caring for him and, at the same time, make use of his ration of supplies. But Teddy soon grasped that his son Kermit would not stand for any such thing, and furthermore, even if Teddy died, his son would most likely insist on the crew carrying his dead body with them. As such, Teddy came to the cold conclusion that lugging around his dead body would be even more of a burden than assisting his weakened, but fully alive, one. Teddy then put any thought of dying out of his mind and struggled to go on. Sadly, much of what he became afflicted with in that South American wilderness would never quite leave his system, and he would have to deal with intermittent bouts of malaria and inflammation for the rest of his life.

Nevertheless, in the end, Teddy and company successfully mapped some five hundred miles of the River of Doubt, and the government of Brazil was so thankful for it that they renamed it the Rio Roosevelt. Ironically enough, by the time of his return to the United States, Teddy Roosevelt found his detractors completely full of doubt, as they were skeptical of whether he had even explored the river at all.

This led to Teddy addressing his skeptics at a conference hosted by the National Geographic Society, in which he went on the record to prove his accomplishments. With this burden unloaded, Teddy prepared himself for the fallout of the 1914 midterm elections. It had been the first contest of his Progressive Party since the 1912 presidential election. Sadly, the results were not promising in the least. With the exception of California, Progressive candidates in every state proved to face complete and abject failure. After hearing of these results, Teddy didn't pull any punches when he surmised, "I should suppose that the Progressive party now should probably disband."

The party had been formed around the larger-than-life figure of Teddy Roosevelt, and it seemed that it could not survive without his guiding light as an active part of it. Teddy, however, had had enough, and he was not willing to inject any new life into the faltering party, confiding at the time, "It will be, from the selfish standpoint, a great relief to me personally when and if they do disband." As far as Teddy was concerned, his days in politics were all but over. However, international portents and the potential of a world war would leave Roosevelt wondering if he could have done more.

Chapter 10 – A World War and a Worried Father

World War One, which was, up until that point, the most expansive war the world had ever known, began over a series of rather localized events. In the summer of 1914, the heir to the Austro-Hungarian throne, Archduke Franz Ferdinand, was paying a visit to Sarajevo when a young Serbian terrorist by the name of Gavrilo Princip shot into the car the archduke and his wife Sophie were riding in.

Both Franz Ferdinand and Sophie would die of their injuries. Austria-Hungary was understandably outraged over what had happened, but in their anger, instead of just punishing the assassin, they seemingly sought wholesale punishment from the Serbian homeland from which Princip hailed. Austria-Hungary handed out a draconian ultimatum to Serbia, which, among other things, demanded that the Serbian government allow an Austro-Hungarian-led investigation and that the Serbs pledge to rid itself of terrorism.

On the surface, it may sound fairly reasonable, but the Serbs considered it to be a gross overreach to have to allow Austro-Hungarians into their territory as they conducted their own private inquiries. Nevertheless, Austria-Hungary persisted and demanded compliance with its terms within 48 hours or else. After this deadline passed without a reply, the war drums began beating.

But what would have been just a skirmish between Austro-Hungarians and Serbians quickly spiraled out of control when Russia sided with Serbia, Germany sided with Austria-Hungary, and Britain and France, due to their participation in the Triple Entente that had them aligned with Russia, joined the growing conflagration as well. With these battle lines drawn, Austria-Hungary declared war on Serbia for its perceived insolence, officially kicking off World War One on July 28th, 1914.

Germany and Austria-Hungary would then link up with Turkey's Ottoman Empire, forging an alliance that would be known as the Central Powers. If Austria-Hungary was even in the least bit justified in its heavy-handed reaction to the archduke's assassination, the actions of wartime Germany would overshadow any credibility Austria-Hungary initially had. Shortly after the hostilities began, Germany invaded neutral Belgium in an effort to create a beachhead against France. They did this to create a path around the heavily defended France/German border, allowing for a more rapid push into France. Not only was this a violation of a neutral nation, which had nothing to do with the conflict, the Germans, frustrated with Belgian resistance, also began to perpetrate horrible war crimes against the populace. If, for example, a Belgian sniper picked off a few German troops, it wasn't uncommon for the commander of that German unit to kill innocent villagers from where that sniper hailed as a kind of reprisal.

Teddy Roosevelt was, at first, hesitant to judge the Germans too harshly. When news of the German invasion first came to his attention in the first week of August, he only remarked, "I simply do not know the facts." But soon enough, he began to believe that the Germans were indeed committing an evil act by invading a neutral nation in the fashion that it did. As he told his friend Arthur Lee, "There is not even room for an argument. The Germans, to suit their own purposes, trampled on their solemn obligations to Belgium and on Belgium's rights."

Ironically enough, within a week of this trespass, Teddy received a message from none other than Kaiser Wilhelm II. Teddy had met Kaiser Wilhelm during his tour of Europe in 1910 and had been impressed with the German leader's hospitality. After the outbreak of World War One, the Kaiser was apparently seeking to shore up support from a man he thought might be an ally. The message recalled the visit they had together and stressed that the Kaiser hoped that Teddy would remain an ally during the "difficult times" that Germany was facing.

Teddy's reply was courteous yet blunt and completely to the point. He declared to the Kaiser's envoy who had given him the message, "Pray thank His Imperial Majesty from me for his very courteous message; and assure him that I was deeply conscious of the honors done me in Germany, and that I shall never forget the way in which His Majesty the Emperor received me in Berlin, nor the way in which his Majesty King Albert of Belgium received me in Brussels."

Without even mentioning the invasion of Belgium directly, Teddy made his displeasure with the belligerence crystal clear. While he was at it, Teddy also made his displeasure with American President Woodrow Wilson pretty clear as well. It wasn't so much anything Wilson did but rather what he didn't do. Teddy was surprised that in the initial days of the invasion, Wilson made no move to at least diplomatically condemn the Germans. Teddy felt that such a stern rebuke would at least cause the Germans to reconsider their actions, but no such condemnation was forthcoming from the Wilson administration. Teddy also criticized President Wilson for what he perceived as a lack of war readiness. It wasn't so much that Teddy wanted to drag America into the conflict, but he felt that the US at least needed to be prepared. If anything, it would help to give the US better clout in the international community when it came to potentially helping to negotiate a solution to the conflagration that had unfolded.

The events that would occur in the spring of 1915 would only further enrage Roosevelt, especially when it came to the leadership stylings of Woodrow Wilson. In May, the Germans amped up their aggression by having one of their submarines sink the British steam liner the *Lusitania*. The ship was blown out of the water, killing over a thousand men—with 128 of them being Americans. Back in 1898, when Teddy was the assistant secretary of the US Navy, the sinking of the USS *Maine* and the loss of a few hundred American lives was enough for America to declare war on Spain.

If Teddy was president instead of Woodrow Wilson, he, no doubt, would have been heading the nation to war for this affront as well. But to Teddy's astonishment, President Wilson seemed ready to take this abuse from the Germans. Wilson famously declared at the time that there was "such a thing as being too proud to fight." In the end, Wilson merely suggested that the Germans apologize, pay for the damages, and promise not to do it again. To Teddy, Wilson, who before being president of the United States had served as the president of Princeton, must have seemed like a school principal rapping one of his pupils on the knuckles and shouting, "Don't do it again!"

Teddy knew the German psyche very well. He knew that if they did it once, they most certainly would do it again. Nevertheless, for the time being, the Germans complied with Wilson's request, leaving Teddy to feel disgusted that the Germans could kill Americans and receive little more than a slap on the wrist.

And Teddy wasn't the only one. As general dissatisfaction with Wilson grew, both the Republican Party and the floundering Progressive Party began to once again look to Teddy Roosevelt as a possible answer to their woes. Could he possibly beat Woodrow Wilson in the upcoming presidential election in 1916? Some believed that he could. But he could only do so if he had both of these factions united together.

It was for this reason that these two supposed separate parties developed a collaborative effort in 1916 that had them both holding their conventions in Chicago at the same exact time and with the same protocol. It was as if they were trying to feel each other out, to see what might happen next. The Republicans ended up rejecting Teddy, however, since the more conservative wing that had backed Taft in 1912 proved unable to move past previous grievances.

This left the Progressives clamoring for Teddy, but Roosevelt knew better. He realized that the odds of him winning in 1916 were even slimmer than they were in 1912, and furthermore, as his health began to decline, he knew he just wasn't up for the hardship such a campaign would entail. The Progressives were obstinate, though, and proceeded to nominate Teddy anyway.

Nevertheless, Teddy still turned them down. And declining their invitation virtually spelled the end for the Progressives as a party. The Republicans, meanwhile, nominated a Supreme Court judge, Charles Evans Hughes, to be their candidate in the election. Initially, Teddy refused to back Hughes, but after considering Hughes's efforts to make the country more prepared for potential war, Teddy eventually came around and decided to stump for the new Republican presidential candidate.

To Teddy's chagrin, Wilson's anti-war stance played out well with a powerful majority of the public, and Wilson was reelected largely on the fact that he kept America out of the war. Nevertheless, shortly into Wilson's second term, he became convinced that there was no other choice but to confront an increasingly belligerent Germany, and war was duly declared on April 6th, 1917.

It was a little later than Teddy's liking, but it still served as vindication all the same. Teddy was reinvigorated by the news and began to make his own preparations for war. He met up with Wilson shortly thereafter and informed Wilson that he could count on him for any aid in the war effort. Teddy especially declared his approval for President Wilson's newly implemented draft, but as a caveat, he asked if he could raise his own volunteer division outside of the mandatory draft.

Initially, it seemed to Teddy that Wilson approved, but shortly after their meeting, Teddy received an official rejection. Teddy believed that such a volunteer force serving as a vanguard to the regular army would be great for boosting enthusiasm. These plans were still rejected all the same. To Teddy's chagrin, there would be no Rough Riders running roughshod in World War One.

Unable to rouse his own troops, Teddy worked to rouse the American people. This he did through writing articles and giving several public speeches. Theodore Roosevelt also committed himself in another way—he had all four of his sons enlist and serve in the war. His sons, Ted Jr. and Archibald, joined up with General John Pershing's expeditionary force. His oldest son, Ted Jr., who himself was married with a family of his own, served with distinction, rising to his father's rank of lieutenant colonel.

Archibald likewise was courageous during the conflict, saving the captain of the infantry unit in which he served and getting wounded in the process. Kermit Roosevelt, meanwhile, fought hard in both France and what was then called Mesopotamia (modern-day Iraq). In the latter of which, Kermit actually fought alongside the British Army. Here, Kermit's experience in inhospitable terrain, from all of the expeditions he undertook with his father, would prove invaluable. Teddy had contacted British Prime Minister David Lloyd George to personally make the arrangements for Kermit's service with the British Army. Teddy told George, "I pledge my honor that he will serve you honorably and efficiently." And he did. But in the midst of all this valor and distinction, it was Teddy's youngest son that would pay the highest price.

At just twenty years old, Quentin had become a pilot and soared through the dangerous skies of the Western Front. It was here that he would meet his end, shot down over France in the summer of 1918. Just a week prior to his death, Teddy was regaled by one of Quentin's letters that related his downing of a German plane. Now, Teddy was on the receiving end of the casualties of war, with his own son perishing in the conflict.

The first clue Teddy received that his son might be in trouble occurred on July 16th when a journalist friend of his named Phil Thompson mentioned that he had a telegram for the *New York Sun* advising to "Watch Sagamore Hill." This was, of course, in reference to Teddy's own residence at Sagamore Hill. His friend was confused by the directive, wondering why sudden scrutiny would be on Teddy's abode.

The ever-intuitive Roosevelt had a good idea, however, and had the sinking suspicion that something wasn't quite right on the Western Front. Teddy looked gravely at his friend and informed him, "Something's happened to one of the boys." Teddy didn't know what it was, but something dreadful most certainly had occurred. The next day, on July 17th, the same journalist returned to Sagamore Hill and confirmed Teddy's worst fear.

As it turned out, Quentin's plane had been waylaid by two German planes and had crashed behind enemy lines. But even as bad as this report appeared, it still did not clarify whether Quentin died in the crash or had been taken prisoner by the Germans. Teddy tried to put on a brave face and offered Thompson an official statement for publication. In it, Teddy, on behalf of himself and his wife, declared, "Quentin's mother and I are very glad that he got to the front and had a chance to render some service to his country, and show the stuff that was in him before his fate befell him."

Nevertheless, despite the brave show he put on, later that day, his personal secretary would recall Teddy in his office struggling to even do routine tasks, with "his voice choking with emotion and tears streaming down his face." Teddy managed to pull it together enough, and the next day, he stood before a Republican state convention in Saratoga to give a speech. The midterm elections were drawing near after all, and it was once again expected of Teddy to galvanize the electorate.

The speaking engagement had been scheduled before Teddy heard the news of his son being shot down, and most would have understood if he had to cancel in light of the circumstances. Teddy wouldn't have it, however, and he insisted on speaking for those who had gathered. In the speech, Teddy was noted to be a little more subdued than usual, but he stayed on message.

Speaking to a matter obviously close to his heart, Teddy declared to those assembled, "The finest, the bravest, the best of our young men have sprung eagerly forward to face death for the sake of a high ideal; and thereby they have brought home to us the great truth that life consists of more than easygoing pleasures, and more than hard, conscienceless, brutal striving after purely material success."

Even with the loss of his son, Teddy would not disavow the need for young men to "face death" in the name of preserving the freedoms Americans held dear. It was just a couple of days after Teddy issued this speech that he received the final confirmation that his youngest son Quentin had indeed perished when his plane was shot down. After Teddy was forced to accept that his son was not returning from the war, he and Mrs. Roosevelt spent the next few months quietly reflecting on their son's life.

The war, meanwhile, was quickly drawing to a close, with the Allies angling to figure out under just what terms Germany should surrender to. American President Woodrow Wilson led the charge with his so-called "Fourteen Points," which outlined what he felt the postwar conditions should be. Teddy, a long-time critic of Wilson, felt that the terms went too easy on Germany, which he viewed as an "outlaw among nations." Teddy felt that nothing short of unconditional surrender would be a slight to the United States. As Teddy himself put it to his old confidant Cabot Lodge, "If construed in its probable sense, many and possibly most of these fourteen points are thoroughly mischievous, and if made the basis of peace, such peace would represent not the unconditional surrender of Germany but the conditional surrender of the United States."

The nation was on the eve of the midterm elections, meanwhile, and Wilson had implored the American public to vote for the Democrats if they approved of how the president handled the war. Teddy was thoroughly disgusted by the apparently partisan tactic. And when he heard of it, he declared, "The President's appeal is a cruel insult to every Republican father and mother whose sons have entered the Army or the Navy."

Perhaps a majority of Americans shared Teddy's sentiment because, on election day, the will of the people appeared to reject President Wilson's overtures. Instead of voting for Democrats, they voted for Republicans in droves, resulting in Wilson's party losing control of both the House and the Senate. All the same, just days after these votes were cast, Germany finally agreed to an armistice, bringing World War One to a close on November 11th, 1918.

Even after the armistice was signed, Teddy still found himself irked by Wilson, annoyed with the idea of him sitting "at the head of the peace table" at the close of the war. He even went so far as to voice his grievances to British Foreign Secretary Arthur Balfour. Writing a letter to remind the British that Wilson's party had just been rejected during the midterm election, Teddy's missive declared, "He demanded a vote of confidence. The people voted a want of confidence, by returning to each House of Congress majority of the Republican Party of which I am one of the leaders."

The idea that Teddy would air such dirty laundry in front of foreign leaders would be deemed by most as highly inappropriate, if not outright illegal. But at any rate, he certainly had one thing right. In the aftermath of both the midterms and the conclusion of the war, Teddy Roosevelt had once again become a leader of the Republican Party. And it wasn't long before the chance of him running in the upcoming 1920 presidential election became an open topic of conversation.

Teddy himself would even decline a stab at running for governor of New York, allegedly to conserve his energy for a potential presidential bid. As he told his sister Corinne at the time, "Corinne, I have only one fight left in me, and I think I should reserve my strength in case I am needed in 1920." This statement was also a pointed indication that Teddy's once boundless wellspring of energy was finally beginning to run dry.

Not only that, but several longstanding illnesses were also beginning to significantly sap his strength. The doctors had recently informed Teddy that he was suffering from a form of inflammatory rheumatism, which had been most likely exacerbated by his rigorous adventures in South America. It was on the very day of the signing of the armistice that ended World War One that Teddy's ailments flared up so bad he was sent to the hospital. Teddy wouldn't be discharged until Christmas Eve.

Teddy seemed to recover, but in order to get through his day, he now depended on a veritable cocktail of painkillers, including a daily dose of morphine. Teddy would live through Christmas and New Year's, managing as best as he could, with many believing he was on the rebound. But after a long day of working on an editorial piece for a newspaper on January 5th, Theodore Roosevelt went to bed for what would be his last night on this Earth.

Before he slept, a nurse who was standing by dutifully injected him with morphine to help him relax enough for slumber. His last recorded words were to his servant, James Amos, when he asked him, "James, would you put out the light." James then observed Teddy sleeping over the next few hours, but around four in the morning, James was alarmed to find that Teddy's breathing began starting and stopping in several rapid bursts.

Around 4:15 a.m., Teddy seemed to stop breathing entirely. James yelled for the nurse, who then, in turn, brought in Teddy's wife, Edith. All three tried everything they could to get the old Rough Rider to start breathing again, but Teddy was beyond their reach.

Teddy Roosevelt passed away on January 6th, 1919, at the age of sixty. Although he had survived battles, an assassination attempt, and jungles on two continents, it was a coronary embolism that ultimately took his life. Even when bullets, tigers, and lions couldn't kill him, a small blood clot in his lungs could.

Two days later, on January 8th, 1919, Teddy's funeral was held in Oyster Bay, New York. The service saw men from all walks of life. Ranch hands to heads of state were all in attendance to pay tribute to the extraordinary life that Teddy Roosevelt had lived. He was gone, but he most certainly wasn't forgotten—and most likely never will be.

Conclusion: Teddy's Lasting Legacy

Teddy once said to walk softly but carry a big stick. And he traveled all over creation practicing what he preached. From his time spent cleaning up corruption as a police commissioner in New York to the Spanish-American War and beyond, he was willing and ready to live by his noble code. Teddy Roosevelt was a man of rare character. Even when his own son perished in World War One, Teddy was quick to declare that the cause was just and that his own sons should not be spared in upholding it. If the cause was worthy enough, Teddy was ready to take part in it.

This was the case immediately before his death, as Teddy was preparing to make one last presidential run in 1920. If he had lived to see the day, one could only speculate what might have happened. Would he have won? It's quite possible he would have. Instead, that honor went to fellow Republican Warren Harding. Although they shared the same party, Harding would be the complete antithesis of Roosevelt in many ways. Harding's administration was corrupt practically from the beginning, with Harding being the pawn of the party bosses who got him elected in the first place. This meant that Harding was very much a part of the "spoils system" that Teddy had fought so hard against. Beholden to those who helped him gain office, Harding filled his Cabinet with those not necessarily best suited for the job, instead choosing political cronies he owed various favors to.

Harding himself would often feel victimized by the political hacks pulling his strings, and he would die in office of a massive (probably stress-induced) heart attack. His death came just prior to the sordid revelations of the Teapot Dome scandal. As it turned out, the Harding administration was in bed with big business, and his administration was taking kickbacks from the oil industry in exchange for drilling access to lands in Teapot Dome, Wyoming, which had been set aside as a naval reserve.

If Teddy Roosevelt knew about all of this, he would have been rolling over in his grave. Not only was Harding's administration engaged in the corrupt abuses of power that Teddy had so long fought against, but President Harding was also allowing companies to drill on land that had been reserved at the behest of the great conservationist himself! It should be noted that it was actually Teddy's successor, President Taft, who signed into law the status of Teapot Dome as a US naval reserve in 1910. Since then, the land had been held as off-limits unless a national emergency called for its use.

This was certainly in line with Teddy's doctrine, which was to conserve land and resources whenever possible. Teddy never imagined that such things would be so easily violated. Perhaps even more galling was the fact that one of the chief architects of the scheme was Albert Fall, a senator from New Mexico who was a former Rough Rider himself. But although Fall had previously been friends with Teddy, he never agreed with him on the concept of conservation. And as soon as his buddy Warren Harding gave him the post of secretary of the interior, Fall was ready to violate the very lands that Teddy had fought so hard to secure. This is incredibly ironic since this was a man that Teddy trusted a great deal. At one time, Teddy described Albert Fall as "the kind of public servant of whom all Americans should feel proud." With what transpired in the few years following Teddy's death, however, it just goes to show how quickly others can try to undo someone else's legacy.

But in the end, this aberration to Teddy's vision was just a momentary blip, and the other sections of the country Teddy had designated as reserves would remain intact. So, too, would his rules and regulations for business and consumer protection. The FDA, for example, which was created under Teddy's watch, remains in place. And Americans are all the better for it. All of these things are crucial to their daily lives, and they can thank Teddy for them. His was a truly lasting legacy that has touched the world in general and continues to have an effect on us to this very day.

If you enjoyed this book, then I'd really appreciate it if you would post a short review on Amazon. I read all the reviews myself so that I can continue to provide books that people want.

Here's another book by Captivating History that you might be interested in

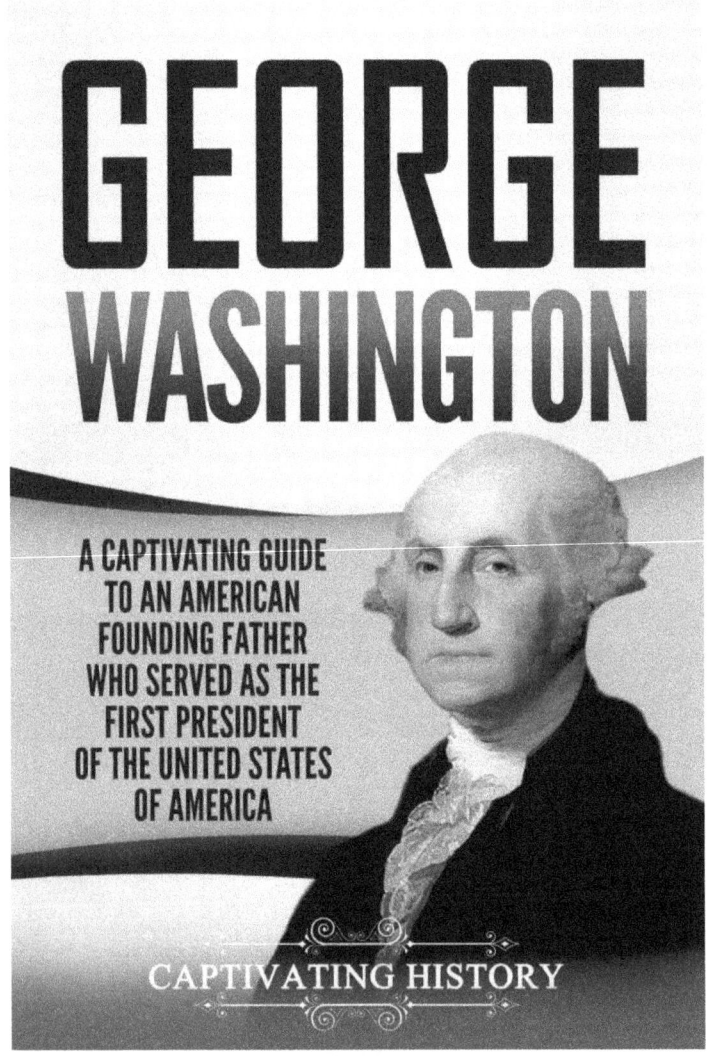

References:

T.R.: The Last Romantic. Brands, H.W.
Theodore the Great: Conservative Crusader. Ruddy, Daniel

Printed in the USA
CPSIA information can be obtained
at www.ICGtesting.com
LVHW090936161223
766669LV00058B/2196